A SEARCH

This book examines what it means to be a Christian in the 1990s. How should Christians apply their faith, show God's love, respond to events, in a world of so many bewildering changes?

How do traditional Christian values, the Authority of the Bible, fit into such a world?

How should the Christian Church relate to other Faiths in multi-faith societies?

The author explores all these matters, drawing on some of the most up-to-date scholarship in these areas, as well as more homely wisdom.

His verdict: Profound social changes call less for a new Christian message than for new ways of presenting it. But he looks at traditional biblical values in the context of changing attitudes towards such things as marriage, homosexuality, race relations, ecumenism, the feminine revolution, violence and the environment. *And in the light of Jesus' radical teaching*.

The author believes that the Bible is speaking to today's situations and that, as ever, God is looking to act in partnership with human beings. But humans have to remember that they are the *junior partners*.

By the same author

What did Jesus Teach?
Denholm Press 1969

A SEARCH

A. Gordon Jones

JANUS PUBLISHING COMPANY
London, England

First published in Great Britain 1993
by Janus Publishing Company

British Library Cataloguing-in-Publication Data
A catalogue record for this book is available
from the British Library

ISBN 1 85756 007 8

Cover design David Murphy
Phototypeset by Intype, London
Printed and bound in England by
Antony Rowe Ltd, Chippenham, Wiltshire

Contents

Preface

In this last part of the twentieth century we are aware that we live in a time of widespread, and sometimes dramatic, educational, religious, racial, sexual and cultural change. This raises acute questions for the Christian Church – questions which it is facing and to which it seeks answers. The overriding question we face is: what, in practice, does being a Christian mean today?

I have tried to live by the Christian Faith – with many failures – all my life; it has meant being engaged in a continuous search for answers to the question: what does my faith say to today's situations? In this book I present some of the answers, or approaches to answers, or uncertainties about answers, that have resulted from my search. In one sense, therefore, this book is a testimony to my own experience. But I hope it is more than that. Just as one of the tasks of the preacher is to try to put into words the faith and the searchings of the congregation of which he or she is a part, and to stir them to engage more eagerly in their own search, so the writer of a book like this hopes he is expressing some of the thoughts of his readers and encouraging them to increase their own efforts to apply the Faith to today.

This is not an autobiography! I refer here not only to my own personal thoughts but those of wiser thinkers than myself. So, far more than being a personal testimony, it is intended to be a discussion-starter in groups. Hence the suggested questions at the end of each chapter.

In Chapter 1 I draw attention to some of the changes – many of them profound – taking place today. In Chapter 2 I discuss our understanding of the Bible – because it is the foundation document of our Faith. In subsequent chapters I attempt to explore what all this might mean with regard to denominational relations; how Christianity and other World Faiths interrelate (now that Britain is a multifaith society); racial relationships; sexual relationships; the changed status of women; and – subjects much in people's minds today – ecology and the environment, and the great responsibility we realise we have because of our advances in genetic understanding and skills – matters of life and death. The final chapters look at Old Age and Violence.

If this book encourages readers to a deeper exploration, it will have served its purpose.

GJ (June 1992)

Acknowledgements

Passages quoted from the Revised English Bible c 1989 by permission of Oxford and Cambridge University Presses

Passage quoted from *Illustrated English History*, G. M. Trevelyan, 1944 by permission of Longman Group UK

Passage quoted from *Human Reproduction – a study of some emergent problems and questions in the light of the Christian Faith*, 1962, British Council of Churches by permission of CCBI Publications

Passage quoted from *The River Within*, Christopher Bryant, 1978, by permission of Darton Longman & Todd Ltd.

1. The Challenge of Today

A Challenge

Everybody who believes in God is a theologian! Theology is the attempt to work out what we understand about God, his nature and his purposes. And many people's theology is undergoing a change today. Much of that change constitutes what some might call a liberalising of theology. Our thinking, as Christian believers, is being challenged at many points. If I mention the Bishop of Durham and Don Cupitt as just two of the Christian thinkers who are trying to help us sort out these challenges, some readers may curl up in disgust. It is certainly true that some of the things they write and say are difficult – and let's admit that sometimes academics don't seem able to say what they mean in straightforward, everyday language! But they are still Christians. And their objective is not to dispense with the Faith but to make it more meaningful in a bewildered and often sceptical age.

Outdated presentation

The trouble is that so many of us 'ordinary' Christians do not feel 'learned' enough to enter into this activity. We feel we are not called to be academic theologians. Fair enough! But that does not let us off our calling to love God with our heart and soul and mind.

The Church has always had its thinkers and they have published reports and discussion papers by the dozen. But to what extent do we take notice of them and try to grapple with what they say? Not to any noticeable extent. And so, gradually and increasingly, Christian churches are coming to be seen by the vast majority of our population as little, remote, enclosed groups of rather odd people who believe things that really are of no concern to modern people: they and their Faith are seen by many as outdated, irrelevant.

Yet here we are, Sunday by Sunday, proclaiming that we have a Gospel – Good News – for all humanity, a message that liberates people from anxiety, depression, guilt, lovelessness, violence and meaninglessness . . . And it would seem that most people couldn't care less. They go their way, anxious, depressed, guilt-laden, loveless, aggressive, wondering sometimes if life is worth living; and sometimes trying all sorts of opiates (instead of our Gospel) which give them a false sense of living a worthwhile life. It is not that our message is worn out. Rather is it that we have not discovered how to present it in the context of the real situation of the last part of the twentieth century.

There have been, in the history of mankind, times when a new wave of human understanding has come, an enlightenment which sometimes has seemed to leave the faithful fearful and, so to speak, in the midst of a frightening storm which is destroying everything familiar. One such time came in the days of the Old Testament Prophets; another when Jesus appeared on the world's stage; another when the Renaissance took place; another when the astronomers discovered a new view of the universe; another when Darwin opened people's eyes to the evolution of life; another in the arrival of the age of sophisticated technology. And now, as the twentieth century draws to its close, another such time is upon us. Our world is not the world of the prophets, nor of Jesus, nor of the seventeenth century, nor of the beginning of the twentieth century. It has changed – and is changing. Alvin Tofler's book, *The Third Wave,*[1] argues that there have been two outstanding revolutions in recent world history – the Agricultural Revolution and the Industrial Revolution. But in our time a new revolution is upon us – the 'third wave' – in which, among other things, the vast corporations and central direction of affairs are giving place to smaller groups with their own political and cultural demands and ideals. This is affecting human relationships in industry, politics, homes. We are all caught up in this third wave. And yet the basic need of human beings – to know they are loved and to know how to love – does not change. The question is: what we know deep in our hearts to be the ultimate purpose of the universe – what does it mean for us *now*?

A 'counter-culture'

To try and answer that question is a challenge, not only to preachers but to *all* church members. For in the end Christian witness is done by all Christian men and women, as they go about their ordinary, everyday lives talking with others and showing by their attitudes and actions what their Christian faith means to them. In his Introduction to The Sermon on the Mount[2] John Stott wrote that young people today are searching for a counter-culture, i.e., a way of living that is different from the unsatisfactory culture, the accepted way of life, of today. They do not look for it in the Church, he said; all they see there is conformation, a kind of comfortable, largely middle-class way. Jesus' Sermon on the Mount, Stott says, offers a counter-culture. Indeed, the theme of the entire Bible is that God is calling his people out from their various nations' cultures. Further, he says, the Sermon on the Mount is the kind of culture that consists of a whole series of contrasts between Christian and non-Christian standards.[3] Christians are to be different, both from nominal church ideas and from the secular world.

The Sermon on the Mount is a complete delineation of the Christian counter-culture. If it could be seen as such by these young people, what a wave of excited joy would flow over them. For me, all this does not mean 'going back to the Bible' in a narrow sense, but going forward from it – the starting-point, the foundation. This should help those who think all the new thinking of today is somehow destroying the true Christian faith. The attempt to 're-think' Christianity is *not* a turning against the Bible, against either the teaching or the life-style of Jesus, but rather the reverse. It is trying to discover what he is really saying to us – what the heart of the Bible is – and then applying it to the innumerable problems of our time.

So, how do you approach the Bible? Some different approaches are discussed in Chapter 2.

References

1. Alvin Tofler (1980) *The Third Wave*. HarperCollins Publishers, London.
2. John Stott (1978), *The Message of the Sermon on the Mount*, pp 15–19. Inter-Varsity Press, Leicester.
3. Matthew, Chapters 5–7.

Questions for Discussion

1. What are your group's views on the kind of life described in the Sermon on the Mount as a 'counter-culture'?
2. How can we discipline ourselves to examine more deeply the ethical teaching of Jesus? In what ways does it challenge so many of our modern attitudes to the purpose of living? How does his teaching help us to grapple with today's problems?

2. In What Sense is the Bible Authoritative?

How Do You Approach the Bible?

Does not so much of the attempt to 're-think' the Christian approach to various modern situations do considerable damage to our conviction that the Bible is 'The Word of God'? Is the authority of the Bible being swept away by our modern thinking? A few comments on this subject are not out of place here.

As you read some of the things I have written later (e.g. about sexual relationships, especially homosexual relations) you may think that the plain teaching of the Bible is being discarded, or at least reinterpreted out of all recognition. This will be a particular cause of anxiety – even anger – to those who are Bible literalists. I can only state my own understanding.

Every religion has its Book or Collection of Books – its Scriptures. Islam has the Qur'an; Hinduism has the Bhagavad-Gita and the Vedas; Buddhism has the Pali Tripita. Judaism has the Tenach (a term derived from the opening letters of the Hebrew words for Law, Prophets and Writings. Christians call it the Old Testament.) And Christianity has the Old Testament and the New Testament. They are all collections of writings which after a long period of time have come to be regarded as containing the basic teachings of the various Faiths. They contain, in written form, each faith's foundation beliefs.

The Bible is our source-book. It covers the *beginning* – the period of history when Judaism developed its understanding of the One God, absolutely good: 'ethical monotheism'. That was a great step forward from the primitive, pagan world of many gods, though, to be fair, it must be said that many of the polytheistic believers also believed in an Ultimate God, but unattainable. And it covers the time when the Christian Faith – which we claim to be the climax of the Judaistic faith – was born and began to grow.

The Bible covers about 1900 years of history. Out of the great number of books written during this time, both Jewish and Christian authorities chose certain books to become 'The Canon' – the accepted body of their religious teaching.

The Bible is not one book; it is a collection of books. The word 'bible' is from the Latin *biblia* – a plural word meaning 'books'. It is a library in which, as in any library, you find many different kinds of literature. The Old Testament contains Myths (old stories like parables containing truth in story-form); Laws of behaviour for individuals, family, society, nation; Proverbs and traditional Wisdom; what we today would call Novels (e.g. Esther and Job); poetry and hymns (Psalms) and a new type of preaching, that of The Prophets, in which the activity and will of God is discerned and spelled out for the current social and political situations. Then there is the History (found in Genesis, Exodus, Leviticus, Numbers, Deuteronomy, the Books of Samuel, Kings, Chronicles, Ezra and Nehemiah). This was written from a particular point of view. All written history is biased in certain directions – and not necessarily untrue on that account, but seen according to the understanding, experience, philosophy and, perhaps, national viewpoint of the writer. (A history of World War 2 reads differently if written by an English or German historian.) The Jews believed they had a special purpose for their existence, so their account of their history is written with that purpose in mind. In the Books of Kings the writers distinguish between the 'good' kings and the 'bad' kings; as a result they may not always be entirely fair to every king. It depends on whether he is seen as furthering people's understanding of God's will or hindering it.

In the New Testament there is a similar variety of types of literature. There are the Gospels. They are not strictly biographies of Jesus, but rather collections of oral traditions about his teachings and actions written down by committed Christians, who recorded and interpreted the words and deeds which struck them most among the things he said and did. The Good News was variously interpreted. Thus Mark represents the Gospel cherished by Christians in Rome – a simple, clear statement of Jesus as God's Son. Matthew is the Gospel cherished by Jewish Christians; Jesus is portrayed as the fulfilment of messianic hopes. Luke represents the gospel as cherished by the gentiles – Christ the Saviour of the whole world, especially the underprivileged and despised people. John presents the gospel in more philosophical and theological terms and undoubtedly develops words of Jesus into long discourses which explain his words. Yet together, the four Gospels give us a consistent portrait of a real, living and strong personality. They give us a marvellous painting, rather than a photograph.

The Acts is Luke's attempt to tell his readers something of the life of the first few years of the Church's existence – tremendously important in highlighting what were the basics of the Christian Faith at its beginning. The Letters (especially Paul's) were the first Christian documents. Reading letters to other people is always enlightening, not only about the personalities of the writers but about the characteristics of the age in which they lived. The New Testament Letters give us vivid glimpses of the problems the young Church faced and the living experience of Christ which was the life-blood of the first Christian communities. (If you want to be convinced of the reality of Jesus's resurrection, don't turn first to the Gospel accounts – read Paul's letters!)

There is one other type of literature found in both Old and New Testaments– Apocalyptic This seems odd and foreign to many people today (Daniel and Revelation are examples) but was popular in the hundred years before and the hundred years after the birth of Jesus. It is a fantastic kind of picture language which expresses for people undergoing extreme persecution the hope of the final triumph of the kingdom of God over the kingdom of the Devil – of good over evil.

The words 'the Bible says . . .' are the end of the search for truth for some people; they are the beginning for others. The first sort of people are variously described as 'conservative evangelicals' or 'fundamentalists'. They believe in the literal truth of every part of the Bible, the inerrancy of all its statements. Those who do not take this approach would be called 'liberals' or 'radicals'. It should be helpful to remember that the aim of both sorts of readers is the same; 'fundamentalists' are looking for *foundations*; 'radicals' are looking for *roots*. The only difference is that foundations are immovable and changeless – though they may rot away – while roots grow and, with dry or wet weather, good, bad or indifferent layers of soil, may change – but they do bear fruit.

Is everything in the Bible true?

We have come to see that there is a developing understanding in the Bible through its 2000 years – understanding of what God is like, what he is doing and telling his human family to do. And that seems to imply a discarding of some beliefs accepted at earlier stages. Indeed we see this happening in the actual Bible writings. For example, one of the earlier Hebrew convictions, based on a sound belief that a man is responsible to God for his actions, was that succeeding generations were held guilty by God for their fathers' sins. Thus, in *Exodus 20:5*, God says: '. . . I, the Lord your God, am a jealous God, punishing the children for the sins of the parents to the third and fourth generation of those who reject me'. This led to a despair summed up in the popular cynical proverb: 'parents eat sour grapes and their children's teeth are set on edge'. But two prophets of a later generation, Jeremiah[1] and Ezekiel, saw the relationship of each person with God at a deeper level. They both refuted this doctrine of inherited guilt and considered the proverb no longer meaningful. Ezekiel reports God as saying: 'What do you mean by repeating this proverb in the land of Israel . . .? As I live . . . this proverb will never again be used by you in Israel. Every living soul belongs to me; parent and child alike are mine. It is the person who sins that will die'.[2] In other words, whilst there is a certain truth in the proverb (i.e. what we do does affect the fate of others) it is not true to the extent that we make them guilty.

Jesus did the same. He had a great respect for the Law of Moses – as was shown when he was angry with the Pharisees for allowing their traditions to take precedence over the Law.[3] Yet he clearly felt free to criticise the Law, to suggest it was incomplete – to change it, if necessary – in the interests of the one Law of Love.[4] The Old Testament said: 'If a man commits adultery with another's wife, that is with the wife of a fellow-countryman, both adulterer and adulteress must be put to death'. But when an adulteress was brought before him by the Pharisees, who quoted this law to him, he said: 'Let whichever of you is free from sin throw the first stone at her'.[5] He was repudiating the harshness of the Law. There are harsh and revengeful sentiments expressed in some of the Psalms – a longing for retaliation against enemies[6] – and they are clearly negated in the teaching of Jesus.

So we cannot say that everything in the Bible is 'true', is 'God's Word'. There is a development of understanding in the Bible. For these reasons I myself find it difficult to say easily that the Bible is 'the Word of God'. It is the words of men, fallible men, with all their cultural prejudices and ignorance. We need to discriminate, to judge what we read by the standard of what Jesus taught, trying to be led by the Holy Spirit and re-interpreting in the light of our modern knowledge and situations. And to some extent, this applies to our reading of the New Testament as well as the Old.

The Authority of the Bible

Yet, time and time again, as we have been reading or listening to the reading of the Bible, something has come right home to us, and we have felt, 'this is the truth'. And we have known that here is a word of God. So I believe that the Bible – both Old and New Testaments – needs to be read with intelligent research, always awaiting the enlightenment of the Holy Spirit. Then it does open our eyes to the authentic word of God. Then it becomes authoritative. The authority of the Bible does not lie in a literal inerrancy, but in the undoubted fact that it is the literature of a people who were continually open to the leading of God's Spirit. Unless we look at the Bible in this way, we are in danger either of rejecting it altogether because we cannot accept some of it, or treating it as an idol to be worshipped. This is bibliolatry. Only One is to be worshipped – God himself. This is not to reject the Bible. I hope that readers will note that all that follows puts the Bible centrally in the efforts to deal with the matters that will be examined.

So now we proceed to some of the realms where there is need for deeper thought; where there is sometimes tension, misunderstanding or outdated convictions; and where Christianity has a tremendous contribution to make if only we will be ready to face up to these things honestly.

But first we need to deal with a domestic matter – the structure of the Christian community itself – and this is the subject of Chapter 3.

References

1. Jeremiah 31: 29–30.
2. Ezekiel 18: 1–4.
3. Matthew 15: 3–9.
4. Matthew 5: 21–23.
5. John 8: 4–7.
6. e.g. Psalms 55 and 58.

Questions for Discussion

1. How important is the Bible in your life? Do you read it privately? Have you a system of Bible-study – e.g. the use of daily Bible notes?
2. What do you understand by 'the authority of the Bible'? In what sense can you call it 'the Word of God'?
3. Why do you think that in the chapters that follow, the Bible is considered an essential part of our efforts to deal with our modern problems?

3. Churches Together in Pilgrimage

Divisions among Christians

The relationships between the various branches of the Christian Church need to be given careful examination if what the Church has to say on other broader matters today is to be heard.

There are, and always have been, differences of interpretation of what Christianity teaches between different groups of Christians; and so denominations and cross-denominational groupings have come into existence. The basics are the same: belief in One God who is Love and has been revealed in innumerable ways and pre-eminently for us in the man who appeared at a particular time in history – Jesus of Nazareth, the man who showed that God cares for all human beings and wants them to enter his kingdom, where his loving will is accepted and done. But this basic message has got mixed up with political and cultural ideologies and, often, with sinful humanity's desire for power. Sadly, that led in past centuries to persecution when so-called 'heretics' (those who did not accept the whole doctrine of the ascendant church) were actually killed.

Those days have passed. But until fairly recently people of one denomination spurned people of another as 'wicked' or 'unbelievers'. I remember how, as a child, I looked at Roman Catholic priests and nuns with a mixture of fear and disgust! That attitude, too, has gone and we rejoice that today local Councils of Churches have Anglicans, Catholics, Methodists, members of the United Reformed Church and Baptists, all sharing ideas and insights –

even though Roman Catholics still do not feel able to share the Eucharist with non-Catholics. We have today seen clearly that the Gospel is one, and that if it is to be proclaimed meaningfully and with effect, it must be seen by the world as one.

A fresh approach to unity

Various schemes of organic unification have been devised this century. Some have worked: the Wesleyan, United and Primitive Methodists came together in 1932, though there are still some who want to remain as they were. The Congregationalists and the Presbyterians (most of them) joined together in the 1970s to form the United Reformed Church. Attempts to join the Church of England and the Methodist Church failed. Perhaps, we are thinking today, organic union is not the best way forward. Maybe differences in forms of worship, and to some extent doctrinal emphases, are necessary, so long as they do not form a barrier against working together. So now another approach to the whole matter is being prepared. It is a movement called 'Churches Together in Pilgrimage'. New 'ecumenical instruments' are being worked out. In 1990 the British Council of Churches ceased to exist and 'the Council of Churches for Britain and Ireland' came into being. That is not just a change of name. For the first time, Roman Catholics are involved. And it is intended that it will not be some remote body which ordinary church members feel has nothing to do with them.[1] It will truly begin at local level – as indeed it already has in the increasing number of local ecumenical projects, the aim of which is that, instead of each denomination in a neighbourhood organising its meetings and efforts with almost no regard for what the other denominations are doing, they will make sure they do as much as possible together. *We*, the local church people, have to do it; not some unknown committee in a London office. In 1987 delegates from all over Britain met at the Swanwick Conference Centre and issued a Declaration which said: 'Our churches must now move from cooperation to clear commitment to each other, in search for the unity for which Christ prayed, and in common evangelism and service to the world.' I remember, last year, hearing Cardinal Basil Hume, head of the Roman Catholic Church in Britain, speaking about the relationship between the churches as marking six ways in which, through the centuries, they have related to each other. To begin with, Cardinal Hume said, there was *Confrontation*. That period of mutual enmity passed and there came *Coexistence*. Then came *Conversation*. Today there is *Cooperation*. Our next step is to be increasing *Commitment* and (he hoped) ultimately *Communion*. That is the Pilgrimage: from Confrontation, via Coexistence, Conversation, Cooperation and Commitment, to Communion. The question we at local level have to ask ourselves absolutely honestly (as churches and as individual Christians) is: 'Where have we (I) got to along the path of the six C's?'

So far, apart from such events as Christian Aid Week and the Week of Prayer for Unity, the 'togetherness' of the churches has usually taken second place in our church programme, in the business of church meetings. Perhaps that has been inevitable. But now we are being challenged to do nothing separately which we ought to be doing together. This is a line of thinking urgently requiring our attention if the Christian message is really to be heard and taken seriously in today's society. All this is called Ecumenism.

But Ecumenism has a wider meaning – one which is discussed in Chapter 4.

References

1. *Churches Together in Pilgrimage* (1989) (British Council of Churches & Catholic Truth Society), London.

Questions for Discussion

1. What part can *our* church play in the 'Churches Together in Pilgrimage' movement described in this chapter? Is it important that we do play our part?
2. To what extent does your church cooperate with other denominations in your neighbourhood? Where have *you* got to along the path of the *six C's*?

4. Christianity and other World Faiths

Are non-Christian faiths heathen superstitions?

The word 'Ecumenism' comes from the Greek *'Oikumene'* which means 'the whole wide world'. So 'ecumenical', we are coming to realise, refers not only to relations between different branches of the Christian Church, but to relations between Christianity and other World Faiths. There are, in Britain today, a million Muslims – followers of the Faith founded by Mohammed. They have several beautiful Mosques, such as those in Regents Park and Whitechapel. There are Buddhists and Sikhs and Hindus, to mention just some of the other Faiths in our country. I have known some British young people who have become Buddhists because they have found something in Buddhism which they could not find in their Christian churches.

Time was when Christians simply wrote off all other faiths as 'heathen superstitions'. The whole aim of the Christian missionary movement was to go out into all the world and make Christians. The basic New Testament text that was the driving-force behind this was: 'Jesus said: "I am the Way, the Truth and the Life. No one comes to the Father except by me" ' (*John 14:6*). And then there were his words: 'Go therefore to all nations and make them my disciples . . .' (*Matthew 28:19*). That seemed clear enough!

Discovering the riches of other Faiths

And yet . . . I once organised a course on 'Christianity and Other World Faiths'. I got a Jewish Rabbi, a Sikh Leader, and Buddhist, Muslim and Hindu priests or leaders to come and tell us briefly about the tenets and practices of their respective faiths. (To be fair, I also got a Christian minister to tell us at one of the meetings about the tenets and practices of the Christian faith!) My word, we learned a few things! And I know we were all deeply impressed with the sincerity, devotion and love shown by all the speakers. I remember that my wife and I had the speakers, week by week, to our house for a meal before the particular meeting at which they would speak. How we warmed to them! Yes . . . I would like Muslims and Hindus and the rest to know about Christ, to get rid of some of the false ideas and prejudices they might have about our Faith; but I was also finding that I, too, had false ideas and prejudices about *theirs*.

In one way, we may long for them all to become Christians, because for me Jesus is the climax, the final, the perfect. On the other hand, we want them to bring us their insights – the deep spirituality within Hinduism, the skill in meditation offered by Buddhists, the fearless witness of all Muslims in regular public prayer, the profound sense of God at work in family and history among the Jews. So what becomes of our missionary work? Of 'no one comes to the Father except by me'?

Let us admit that we struggle with these questions and do not have a clear answer. So far as missionary work is concerned, I am sure missionaries are required – to go and offer their skills and experience to the Christian Churches in Africa, India and the Pacific: churches which are now self-governing, autonomous. To go as partners. But no longer to go with the simplistic idea of 'taking Christ to the heathen'. The purpose, rather, is to share with Christians – yes, and with Muslims, Hindus, Sikhs and Buddhists – the task of serving needy communities, fighting injustice, and above all doing what *all* religions do – seeking to open the eyes of humanity to the spiritual dimension of life. For the real enemy of mankind is not some other religion, but the hard, materialistic secularism that enslaves mankind and fosters what is, in the end, a deep pessimism, a sense of ultimate meaninglessness in life.

This is a task that has inherent difficulties, especially when the particular faith has become a cultural, political thing. This seems to have happened with the fundamentalist Muslims and is creating sharp tensions. The desire for friendship, for dialogue, must be made, not only by Christians to others, but by the others to Christians.

I would go so far as to say that Jesus did not come to make people 'Christians', but rather to enable them to become full 'humans', as God intended people to be – fulfilled, liberated from fear and hate. And insofar as other world faiths are seeking the same end – Buddhism with its aim of Nirvana, Islam with its Law of a merciful Allah in the Koran, and so on – we are not their rivals, but their partners. Still missionary work is necessary, still missionary giving is required, but in a deeper, wider sense.

But what about 'no one comes to the Father except by me'? I remember, years ago, some young people in my church asking me about this. I think my answer was – and continues to be – something like this: Jesus did not say 'No one comes to God except by me'. It was the word 'Father' that was crucial. The context of Jesus' words was the narrow and limited world of the Roman Empire. They did not know about the great faiths of India, for example, at that time. They *did* know about the pagan emperor-worship of Rome, the all-too-human gods and goddesses of Greece – yes, and the harsh, legalistic interpretation of belief in God of some of the scribes and Pharisees. Those ways of worship most certainly did not lead people to trust in a loving God. It was Jesus and his teaching, and ultimately his self-sacrifice on the cross, which could open their eyes to a God who cared and forgave and set free – and could rightly be called 'Father'.

In a way, this is still true. All the world faiths believe in God, or the Ultimate which we call 'God'. But Christ alone has spoken of a God who so loved the world that he comes fully into human life and shares its suffering. A suffering God? That is Christianity's contribution. It is when the truth of that comes home to people that they have really 'come to the Father'. But this does not mean that if you are a faithful Hindu, you have to give up your faith, the faith in which you have been nurtured. It means, rather, that your faith will be enriched. Think of Mahatma Gandhi; he was a faithful Hindu until the day of his death. And yet he deeply respected, indeed loved, Jesus. I would not have had him different.

There are three approaches Christians can make to other Faiths. They are termed exclusivist, inclusivist and pluralist.[1]

Exclusivist, Inclusivist or Pluralist?

The Exclusivist approach means that Christians are so sure that their Faith is not only the best but also the only genuine Faith, that they must condemn all other Faiths. This was an attitude held by most Christians right up to the beginning of this century; it is still the attitude of strict fundamentalists (as, indeed, *mutatis mutandis*, it is for fundamentalist Muslims). For my own part, having read a good deal about other Faiths and having had relationships in particular with Jews – and with members of other Faiths occasionally – I cannot be an Exclusivist.

The Inclusivist approach shows friendship and sympathy to people of other Faiths, but assumes that all that is best in them is really Christian. Without knowing it, they are worshipping Christ. I see the cogency of this approach. Adherents of other Faiths sometimes hold the same approach to those not of their religion; Hindus will happily include Jesus among their saints. I have often felt in the adherents of other religions much of the same spirit that I discern in Christianity. But to suggest that really and truly, despite their allegiance to, say, Mohammed or Gautama, they are worshipping 'the hidden Christ', and, that, although ignorant of the fact, they are Christians, is lacking in respect to them and seems extraordinarily condescending. Those of us whose religious experience is centred in Jesus Christ and who know that we owe all things good to him, may tend towards Inclusivism, but I cannot help feeling that it is somehow artificial, unfair and evasive.

The Pluralist approach accepts that there are many paths to God – and from God to mankind. This does not mean that all religions are necessarily of equal worth, and I am willing to argue about various doctrines. But I will humbly acknowledge their truth for those who hold to their own Faith. I know this is a position full of difficulties; what does this do to the Christian conviction of the finality of Christ's revelation, to the doctrines of the Atonement? (I am helped here by my own rejection of some of the theories of the Atonement which have seemed to suggest that Jesus had to die to change God's mind from judgement to mercy. It is surely not a case of a vengeful God who was somehow changed into a merciful God because of a death in the first century. Rather do I see Christ's death as a great flash of lightning which lit up what had always been the case – the love of God for all people – and which has changed the minds of millions of human beings so that they can now know they are liberated from their guilt and despair.) The difficulties remain, but they should be occupying our hearts and minds very searchingly today.

The world needs the gifts offered by all Faiths. God speaks in many ways to people of different cultures and histories. No longer can we say (as the Roman Catholics once did, but not any more): 'No salvation outside the Church'. I have been a member, in recent years, of a local Council of Christians and Jews and also of a local Council of Faiths. I have learned so much and made such creative relationships. My next-door neighbours were Jews – a loving and lovable couple. I met the husband outside our door one Good Friday. I said to him: 'Happy Passover, Ron!' He said to me: 'Happy Easter, Gordon!' And it was as if the spirit of Moses and the spirit of Jesus passed between us. The world needs what we all have to give, if it is to be saved from the greed, the violence, the putting up of barriers, that could one day destroy us all. Said the Founder of my Faith: 'He who is not against us is on our side.'[2] And, in his humility, he meant by 'on our side' the God he sought to reveal.

References

1. Alan Race (1983), *Christians and Religious Pluralism*. SCM Press Ltd, London.
2. *Mark 9:40*.

Questions for Discussion

1. Is an attempt to understand and accept other World Faiths a betrayal of our complete commitment to Jesus Christ?
2. What are your views on religious education and morning assemblies in day schools?

5. Race Relations

Racial tensions

Closely associated with the question of other Faiths, there is a topic that threatens the world unless we face it squarely: race relations. Concern about this subject varies from one area of Britain to another. It may not be much on the minds of some of the inhabitants of Herne Bay; it is very much on the minds of the inhabitants of Herne Hill, near Brixton, in South London; it may mean little in Eastbourne; it means a great deal in the East End.

Time was when people of the white races hardly ever met up with people of other races. If they did, the other races were seen as inferior, just useful as servants. Today the world has shrunk, though so often people's ignorance, fear and prejudice have not. In Britain today people are of mixed race. (Mind you, we always have been – there are Norman, Saxon and Roman strains in us all!) But with the mixing of the races goes a new kind of pride – or fear – that can lead to mutually aggressive, hostile stances, with people of different races eager to retain and demonstrate their unique characteristics, whether religious or cultural. So the contradiction has arisen. This one nation now sees itself as a multiplicity of nations. In some ways relations between the racial groupings in Britain today are like the relations between the various Christian denominations two or three hundred years ago. Sometimes they lead to violence, racial riots; often to a group's withdrawal from people of a colour other than their own into ghettos, with a sort of Alf Garnett approach by whites to blacks and browns – an approach sometimes reciprocated by the latter groups.

Should our aim in a multiracial society be to eradicate all differences – to attempt the impossible task of pretending we are all the same and should forget our various cultural and ethnic backgrounds? Such an attempt is not only impossible; it also fails to acknowledge the value of the rich variety there is in humanity; each race has its own particular gifts to offer. Paul's image of the body helps us here. Speaking of the gifts of the Spirit, he did not declare we should all have the same gift. 'There are varieties of activity, but in all of them and in everyone the same God is active . . . a body is not a simple organ but many . . . The eye cannot say to the hand: "I do not need you . . ." ' (*1 Corinthians 12:6, 14, 21*). Of course Paul is referring to the Church, but it applies also to the whole body of humanity. It follows that in any society there is a place for separate racial groups pursuing their particular interests. But all too often this, in practice, has meant suspicion and enmity between the groups – the setting up of barriers of fear and prejudice. The differences are there for the sharing of cultures and insights, but so often they have been used to cut off understanding, to the mutual impoverishment of all.

Getting to know one another

We know that this won't do. We are one human species – varied indeed in race and culture – but all (in biblical language) 'made in the image of God'.[1] To despise, hate, reject or ignore those of our brothers and sisters who differ from us in some respects is to despise the image of God. And that is blasphemy – the 'sin against the Holy Spirit' (see Mark 3:22–29). There is an increasingly urgent need for us to try and understand other races, their history, their culture. This is certainly true in the matter of how we worship God. One approach to God is what you may find, say, in Canterbury Cathedral's Evensong – a solemn procession along the nave consisting of demure choirboys and a slowly moving clergyman preceded by a solemn banner-bearer – but it is not the only way to approach God. If Archbishop Tutu leads his people in worship by dancing and waving his hands – that is, equally, an approach to God. Understanding of cultural background is required. Personal knowledge of individual members of other races and cultures is required. Ask yourself: do I know anyone of a race or culture other than mine by his or her name? When you can address another person by name there is immediately a bond forged which overrides differences in colour, shapes of faces, ways of pronouncing words. And the things which show us to be basically the same become evident – the human smile, the human tear, the handclasp or hug, the exchange of ideas. How good it was for me to have as a steward in a church of mine a Ghanaian. How we talked and laughed and worked together; and all was made the more meaningful by my having lived and worked in Ghana where differences in such things as colour seemed to go unnoticed.

And all these things should lead us to see that the Christian Church has a unique opportunity. The membership of many churches – certainly most town churches – today consists of people of several races. Different in their approaches to many things, but one in their common love of God. The 'Faithful and Equal' programme being widely discussed in the Methodist Church urges that more black people should be drawn into the active life, and leadership, of churches. But not so that we can say, rather smugly: 'we do give black people opportunities and are making sure that there are more black people elected as representatives, for instance, to the Methodist Conference;' but because we have realised that both black and white have so much to offer. In the discussion on this subject in the 1990 Conference a young black woman, who was a representative for one of the Districts, expressed this feeling when she said that although she realised that her contribution to Conference was as important as anyone else's, it would have been 'two hundred per cent more wonderful' if she could believe in her heart that she was not present because someone saw the colour of her skin first, and her as a person second.

How we need humility! Why should so-called 'white' be more 'normal' than black or brown or yellow? It was a valuable experience I had some years ago when, travelling in my work to a remote African village, I visited an African woman in her home. She had a little child beside her. Seeing me, the child burst into tears! The woman was apologetic; she said: 'he always cries the first time he sees a coloured person'. Coloured? Of course; I was pink, not the proper and normal colour of brown. What an enrichment of our human life awaits us when we discover that

> In Christ there is no east or west,
> In him no south or north.
> All Christian souls are one in him
> Throughout the whole wide earth.[2]

References

1. See Genesis, Chapters 1, 2 and 3.
2. J. Oxenham, *Hymns and Psalms*, p. 758. The Methodist Publishing House, Peterborough.

Questions for Discussion

1. The habits and values of the various races differ from one another in some respects. Mention some of them. What have we all in common and how can they be recognised and used positively?
2. Many, perhaps most, churches today have both 'black' and 'white' members. This is a great advantage in a society where the races tend to keep apart from one another. So what, in our churches, can we do together to fight against racism?

6. Sexual Relationships Today

Has sexual morality broken down?

If relations between the races is a vitally important subject to face as Christians today, of equal importance is relations between the sexes. There was once an apparently clear-cut Christian understanding of sex and sexual relationships – with marriage as the context within which sexual activity at its physically profoundest was to be contained, and seen as a binding contract (summed up in the words: 'What God hath joined together man must not separate'.[1] This is no longer accepted by millions – including many younger people who live upright and genuinely Christian lives.

A woman wrote to me recently, bringing me up to date with her family story. I had last seen her as a little child, a member of a loving and truly Christian family. Her letter showed me clearly that the love and Christian Faith were still very central to her life. She wrote that she was divorced; 'but I am now very happy living with a man whom I love dearly.' (I take that to mean they are not married.) Thirty years ago I should have been distressed and shocked and might have assumed she had now rejected her Christian upbringing. But I found that I did not feel like that at all when I read her letter. We have a different perception of sexual relationships nowadays. Is that a good thing or a bad? – a progression or a recession?

We all know, I suspect, or have in our own families, young people who 'live with their partner' openly and with no sense of guilt. They are loyal to one another, completely monogamous.

And one has to add that their non-married state probably makes things financially easier for them. They may decide to marry when children arrive. They are not against legal marriage but they do not see it as the *sine qua non* of sexual partnership. Is there significance in the change of name of the Marriage Guidance Council to Relate?

What has happened? Many things. Sex is no longer seen as 'sinful'. Debating in the 1990 Methodist Conference the Report of the Commission on Human Sexuality, the chairman of the committee said: 'Sexuality is not a peripheral matter; it lies at the core of our humanity, and there is, perhaps, no other area of human life where we can hurt one another so deeply or bring greater joy and fulfilment into each other's lives.' People's (and especially younger people's) approaches to sexual relationships are more open and not seen as something to be kept entirely within the context of legal marriage. Add to this the increasing number of marriages that fail, and the 'safer sex' now available, and marriage is not seen so sharply as the solely acceptable context of the full sexual partnership. However, just as many of these partnerships break down as the more 'official' ones.

Sadly, many relationships do break up. The number of one-parent families has greatly increased. And the question arises: are the children now missing full, physical, mental and spiritual nurture? Do they not need, by nature, what *both* father and mother have to give them? These are some of the questions the present situation raises. At least, it is good that the unmarried mother is no longer an object of contempt and the child born out of wedlock is no longer called 'a bastard'.

To marry or not to marry?

I do believe that the married state is the best for sexual and family relationships at their most intimate. But before dismissing all this change as 'immoral', we should realise that among many – most – of today's young people, there *is* a moral code. They are not saying that today in sexual relationships 'anything goes'. They would strongly condemn promiscuity. (Someone has rather amusingly said that we live in the age of 'serial monogamy' – you are completely faithful to the partner you have at the moment!) Sex is not to be seen, most would agree, just as a game to be indulged in. It has to be seen as the instrument – the servant – of a loving relationship. The Report of the Human Sexuality Commission stated: 'We reject any and every sexual expression which involves violence, intimidation, or the abuse of children, women or men.'[2] (I shall refer to this again a little further on.)

Homosexuality

Closely related to the matter of relations between the sexes – and really a part of it – is the question of homosexuality and homosexual activities. Are sexual relations between two males or between two females wrong? A literal reading of the Bible has led most Christians in the past to say they are. We look at a few quotes from the Bible on this subject:

> 'You must not lie with a man as with a woman; that is an abomination.' (*Leviticus 18:22.*)
> 'If a man has intercourse with a man as with a woman, both commit an abomination. They must be put to death . . .' (*Leviticus 20:13.*)

In *Genesis, 19* there is the story of two guests who stayed the night in Lot's house in Sodom. The men of Sodom demanded: 'Where are the men who came to you tonight? Bring them out to us so that we may have intercourse with them.' Lot replied: 'No, my friends, do not do anything so wicked.' Then he added: 'Look, I have two daughters, virgins both of them; let me bring them out to you, and you can do what you like with them.' So Lot, it seems, who regarded the men's demand as 'wicked', did not so regard the alternative he offered – the raping of his daughters! Was the one immoral and the other not? I would suggest that *both* alternatives were wicked; both were forms of rape, that is the sexual intercourse by one without the consent of the other. Note this: it must come into any discussion of sexual relationships, whether they be heterosexual or homosexual.

To complete the biblical references, we turn to Paul. In *Romans* he is describing the immorality of much of Roman society. He refers to those who 'have exchanged the truth of God for a lie . . .' (1:25). ' . . . Among them, women have exchanged natural intercourse for unnatural; and men too, giving up natural relations with women, burn with lust for one another; males behave indecently with males . . .' (26–27).

Sex and Love

Daunting texts, these, for any who look for a more compassionate approach to the subject of homosexuality. Yet (to return to the point I touched on two paragraphs back) we have to put them into their context. Then you can see that they are primarily protests, not so much against sexual practices as against violence and promiscuity. What makes sexual practices 'sinful' is not so much the practices as the attitude involved. A young couple live together outside marriage; but they are faithful to each other and it is love which draws them together. A couple of homosexuals live together and it is love which draws them together and they are faithful to each other. There is nothing of a 'sexual orgy' in them. Sex is, for them, an instinct which is seen as the instrument of a loving relationship. Jesus' attitude to 'fallen' women and Paul's remarkable description of the real nature of love – and what happens to the most splendid virtues when love is absent (*1 Corinthians 13*) – give pause for thought. Paul lists many of these virtues and adds (*verse 3*): 'But if I have no love, I am nothing'.

We all possess 'instincts' and the accompanying instinctual emotions: self-preservation (and its accompanying emotion of fear); need for food (and hunger); sex (and its need for physical expression). The instincts are morally neutral. They become 'evil' when they are separated from love, from compassion, from genuine relationship. Self-preservation then becomes destructive carelessness of the needs of others; the need for food becomes gluttony and greed; social needs turn into gangsterism; sex becomes rape. They are instincts for good rather than evil when they are the servants of loving relationships. Of course, they all require self-control. And this, I think, has to be very much in our minds today as we try to sort out the problems related to sex. Are the lessons on sex given in day schools sufficiently alert to this? To tell a child about sex is not just to describe to him or her the details of human physical anatomy; central to all of it should be careful instructions about relationships – giving as well as receiving.

Marriage defended

For what they are worth, here are my own feelings at present on these topics. I believe marriage is the normal context for complete sexual activity. In marriage an open declaration has been made to society, which makes for stability in that society. And if the marriage has been contracted in the context of the Christian Faith, it is seen as a gift from God and an offering, in return, to God. The case for marriage is well put in the following words:

> One of the urgent tasks of the human race is to humanise the powerful sex drive. This drive, inherited from our animal ancestors and essential for the propagation of our species, needs to be humanised by bringing it under the sway of a caring love that seeks personal intimacy more than physical delight and the good of the other for his or her own sake. Marriage, in all its varied forms, is the institution built up to safeguard humanity, to prevent socially destructive sex rivalry and to protect the needs of children.[3]

But marriage as we see it today is changing. The position of women – no longer seen as inferior to men – has a great deal to do with the change. There may be greater changes still to come before a genuine, modern form of marriage is discovered. In the meantime, I will not condemn young people who 'live together' – though I'd like to be able to discuss things with them!

What is happening to family life?

It is relevant here to consider briefly the changes taking place in family life. For many years 'the family' has been generally thought of as a compact, closely-knit group consisting of mother, father and their children. Mother cares for the home, father earns the money, the children are safe and happy. All this is changing; mother goes out to work, and the children, as they grow up, are more independent, having part-time jobs, money of their own, and many away-from-home interests. There is often a consequent loss of close relationship, increasing conflicting interests and sometimes the breakdown of the home. The sad plight of large numbers of young homeless people sleeping rough on the streets is a sign of this.

But the changes are not necessarily all loss. The 'nuclear family' has had its failings. Very close family ties can become selfish, exclusive of others. People can become careless of those not within their immediate family circle – the unmarried, the single parent. If what is happening today can be understood and responded to, then the gift of caring may be extended to the wider community. Close family ties are important, but only if they are seen as a preparation for the wider life of the family of mankind.

What was the teaching of Jesus on the family? He was a Jew and knew the importance of the family held together by ties of blood. Some of his parables were based on parent-children relationships. He was angry with those Pharisees who allowed the law of Corban to enable them to neglect the needs of aged parents. He remembered the lonely state of his mother as he died on the cross and commended her into the care of his disciple, John (*John 19:26*). But he also recognised how narrow and limiting such family life could become. When his family went seeking him – doubtless anxious for his welfare – and his disciples told him his mother and brothers were outside asking for him, he replied: ' "Who are my mother and brothers?" And, looking round at those who were sitting in the circle about him, he said, "Here are my mother and my brothers. Whoever does the will of God is my brother and sister and mother" ' (*Mark 3:20, 21, 31–35*). A family, for Jesus, was to be a centre of love, but not an enslaving love. The changing situation in relationships today may, if interpreted according to the mind of Jesus, bring that to pass.

Responsible homosexual relationships

Concerning homosexuality, some people think of it as a disability, their view being that the very physical make-up of our bodies – male and female – indicates what seems to be the 'natural' way of physical sexual activity, each giving and receiving what each sex alone can offer. If this view is taken, is it a sin for such a 'disability' to be used so that it does not become a handicap? To take a parallel, I have worked in a village where there is a community of physically disabled people – many of them young, many born disabled. But I did not see them as 'handicapped'. The work provided for them, the ingenious apparatus that enabled them to overcome their disability, and the courage and ingenuity they possessed, actually made their disability a means to a full life, not the negation of it. Is there a parallel here to what so many faithful and loving homosexual partners have done with their 'disability'?

But others of us do not see it as a disability but simply as a different orientation of the sexual instinct. In that case someone engaged in homosexual activity is not seen as 'making the best of a bad job' but as giving expression, in his or her situation, entirely legitimately, to what is his or her true nature. A remarkable 'Heart of the Matter' TV programme on BBC 1 in October 1989 showed how, in Denmark homosexual men or lesbian women, may now be joined in legal partnership, with most of the same rights as heterosexual marriage gives. In Denmark, now, such partnerships are becoming as acceptable as the man-woman partnerships; though the Church has not yet felt able to celebrate the making of such partnerships in a church service. It was a thought-provoking programme indeed!

References

1. *Matthew 19:6.*
2. *Report of the Commission on Human Sexuality* (1990), c/o Methodist HQ, London.
3. Christopher Bryant (1978), *The River Within*, p. 64. Darton, Longman and Todd, London.

Questions for Discussion

1. In its effort to take account of today's widely accepted more 'liberal' approach to sexual relationships, is this chapter guilty of weakening or even denying the basic Christian understanding of sexual morality?
2. What are the views of members of your group on homosexuality? Is it a disability? Are homosexual activities sinful?
3. There is an increase in the number of people today who openly deny the necessity of marriage as the only proper environment for sexual intimacy. What are your views on this?

7. The Feminine Revolution

Male domination

So far I have only briefly referred to the place of women, as women, in today's world. But that, too, is a topic not to be evaded as we try to rethink the implications of our Faith at the end of the twentieth century. What about the 'feminine revolution'? For centuries, humankind has lived in a male-dominated society. The woman has so often been seen as the 'tool' of man's needs and desires: the weaker sex, the obedient wife; the companion, indeed, of the man, but always so that *his* position, *his* power, *his* importance can be highlighted. What, let us ask, is the Bible's attitude to women? We must always remember, when 'searching the scriptures', that they were written at particular times and in terms of the predominant cultures of those times. Our job is to get below the cultural framework to that which is basic truth. We have to adopt this approach with both Old and New Testaments.

The Bible's attitude towards women

So far as the cultural framework is concerned, the inferior place woman takes to man shows itself frequently. Take a few examples. In the *Genesis* story of creation, Eve is made out of one of Adam's ribs; she is the one who tempts him to eat the forbidden fruit; and her punishment: 'I shall give you great labour in child-bearing;

with labour you will bear children. You will desire your husband, but he will be your master.' (*Genesis 3:16*).

In *Proverbs* there is a description of the ideal wife. It is positive and full of praise but, notice, that is because of her serving her husband and children: 'She rises while it is still dark and apportions food for her household.' Interestingly and surprisingly, she has a job outside her home! 'After careful thought, she buys a field and plants a vineyard out of her earnings. She sets about her duties resolutely and tackles her work with vigour. She sees that her business goes well . . .' Splendid! – but it is all done to make life good for her husband, so that 'Her husband is well known in the assembly where he takes his seat with the elders . . .' (*Proverbs 31:15–17, 23*). And I think the final verse in this passage (*31:31*) indicates the same thing – her husband is able to go and talk with his friends at the city gates knowing all is being looked after at home: 'Praise her for all she has accomplished; let her achievements bring her honour at the city gates.' It is a strongly masculine description of what makes the good woman!

In the New Testament we find Paul writing within the Greek-Roman cultural framework: (*1 Corinthians 11:3–5*): 'But I wish you to understand that, while every man has Christ for his head, a woman's head is man . . . A man who keeps his head covered when he prays or prophesies brings shame on his head; but a woman brings shame on her head if she prays or prophesies bare-headed; it is as bad as if her head were shaved . . .'

Here is the writer of the Letters to Timothy:

> (Women's) role is to learn, listening quietly and with due submission. I do not permit women to teach or dictate to the men; they should keep quiet. For Adam was created first, and Eve afterwards (*1 Timothy 2:11–13*).

And of the letter to the Ephesians:

> Wives, be subject to your husbands as though to the Lord; for the man is the head of the woman . . .' (*Ephesians 5:22–24*).

I imagine that most of us reject all this. And if anyone declares that in doing so we are 'rejecting the Word of God', I say: read on in that Ephesians passage (Chapter 6, verse 5): 'Slaves, give single-minded obedience to your earthly masters . . .' Well – we certainly reject *that*. We reject the assumption that slavery is right;

as Christians we know it is *wrong*. If, therefore, we reject this command as something arising out of the cultural setting of that time – and later to be rejected – so we have the right to reject the cultural setting that led to a wrong attitude, in many ways, to women.

But now look more closely at the basic biblical attitude to women. In the creation story we read: 'God created human beings in his own image; in the image of God he created them; male and female he created them' (*Genesis 1:27*). The image of God is *both* male and female. Then consider Jesus' attitude of love, friendship and respect towards women. Throughout the gospels we notice it. He had no hindrances in himself to prevent his speaking alone with a Samaritan woman; he obviously had a warm relationship with Mary Magdalene. And even Paul, in that very passage about the wife's subjection to the husband, goes beyond that to: 'Husbands, love your wives . . . The husband must love his wife as his very self.' (*Ephesians 5:25, 33*).

The Bible is not lacking, by any means, in stories of outstanding women leaders – Deborah the judge; the strong mothers, Rebecca and Rachel; the prophetess Huldah. The home of Lydia became the base for the Christian work in Philippi (*Acts 16:14, 15*). In his letters Paul sometimes refers to women in obvious positions of leadership. In his letter to the Roman Christians he writes: 'I commend to you Phoebe, a fellow-Christian who is a minister in the church at Cenchrea . . . support her in any business in which she may need your help, for she has herself been a good friend to many, including myself' (*Romans 16:1–2*). And there were Priscilla and Mary and Persis and Julia (Romans 16:3, 6, 12 and 15). In all these texts – though it is partially hidden by the culture of the time – there is a recognition of the absolute equality of women with men. Indeed, at one point Paul roundly declares, cutting through all the customary attitudes: 'There is no such thing as Jew and Greek, slave and freeman, male and female; for you are all one person in Christ Jesus' (*Galatians 3:28*).

Equality of male and female

Sadly, this basic understanding got buried again, under male domination, so that for centuries (and still to some extent today) the woman has been pushed down. No longer can this be accepted. The masculinist bias of Christian theology and the idea of a male God is being vigorously challenged. Of course, there are differences between the sexes (and most of us would say 'vive la difference!') But the difference means that the respective gifts of the sexes can now be used equally to enrich our understanding and our life.

Efforts are being made to make our language less male-orientated. This is not easy. It is difficult to know what to do with our normal use of the pronoun 'he' for God. I was delighted, when in Ghana, to find that one word they use for God means 'the father-mother God'. And there are biblical references to God which point to his 'femaleness'. There are indications in the Old Testament of the mother-like love of God; God says to the Jews: 'As a mother comforts her son so shall I myself comfort you . . .' (*Isaiah 66:13*). And Jesus, who, as a human being, clearly had to be one sex or the other, once referred to himself with a feminine analogy: '. . . How often have I longed to gather your children, as a hen gathers her brood under her wings . . .' (*Luke 13:34*). If it is true that we are made in the image of God, then it follows that in him there is both femaleness and maleness. The language difficulties do remain, nevertheless. Brave efforts have been made to amend the wording of some hymns: 'Good Christians all rejoice' has replaced 'Good Christian men rejoice'; the word 'person' is often used where 'man' once was. Care with our language is certainly important and a good sign of our times.

Our new recognition of the equality of the sexes does indeed create some situations which can appear daunting. For example, marriage is changing, with new freedoms for a wife and new responsibilities for a husband. This may not be easy to achieve, but undoubtedly, in time, it will be a great enrichment of the total life of a family.

Ordination of women priests

Then, of course, there is the problem which exercises the Church of England especially today, concerning the ordination of women as priests. The ordination of women was a 'battle' fought and won in the Methodist and other free churches many years ago. Many of us male ministers can testify to the enrichment of our ministry and the whole life of a church and circuit by the presence of women colleagues – their guidance, their insights. We watch with sympathy – and some impatience – as the Anglicans struggle with what is for them still a divisive problem. I believe that the Christian Church has suffered grievously as a result of its male domination. I know that its witness and devotional life is being wonderfully enriched as that domination vanishes. In a time of personal crisis, some years ago, I shared my problem with a friend of mine, the Mother Superior of a Convent. I told her I would rather 'make confession' to her than to a priest. She was a bit shocked. For goodness sake, why?!

Why two kinds of human being?

Why did God create two kinds of human being – men and women? For the purpose of continuing the human race? Presumably he could have devised some other method. For the safeguarding of children in a family as they grow up? Yes, that is fundamental. But I believe it was basically so that humans could be released from solitariness, from static thinking, from a 'one-eyed' view of existence, from being tethered within a monotonous and monomanic system of judging the meaning of life. We were created men and women for the purpose of the sharing of our respective gifts, for love at its most outgoing and non-self-centred. He did not create two kinds of human being in order that one should dominate the other! I read the opening words of Brian Wren's hymn[1] as not merely applying to the occasion of a marriage, but to the whole of human relationships:

> 'As man and woman we were made
> That love be found and life begin'.

Life – physical, mental and spiritual. There may be no marriages in the next world. I am sure there will be that fullness of life which men and women together have discovered.

References

1. Brian Wren, *Hymns and Psalms,* no. 364. The Methodist Publishing House, Peterborough.

Questions for Discussion

1. What does 'the equality of the sexes' mean? Identity? Or the mutual giving and receiving of each of the sexes' unique contribution to full human life?
2. Why do you think the Anglicans have such difficulty in the matter of the ordination of women as priests?

8. Partners in Creation

Concern about the environment

Subjects of immense importance today are the Environment and Ecology. Let's define those words. The Environment means 'surrounding objects, regions or conditions'. Ecology means 'the study of the interaction of our world and how we affect or are affected by it.' There is such intense and widespread interest in these matters today that you might think they do not need to be included in this book. There are so very many books and leaflets available; so many TV programmes devoted to the environment; so many newspaper articles about water pollution, oil-slicks, deforestation causing deserts, food poisoning, dumping of rubbish and nuclear waste in unsuitable places, the spoiling of the countryside by cutting new roads or channel tunnel rail links in places of natural beauty.

Everybody has views on these matters. Government and local councils are concerned. A new parliamentary party has come into existence, the Green Party, although all the other parties swear they are 'green' too! It is a technical problem, a social problem. So, does religion come into it at all? In any case, what can a local group of church members do about it – except to join in the general grumble?

What they can do is to try and discover what is the basic theological significance of all this; in short, what it means to speak of God as the Creator and human beings as his partners in creation.

God the Creator

'In the beginning God created . . .'[1] That is the first sentence in the Christian's Resource Book. 'I saw a new heaven and a new earth . . .'[2] Those words come in the final pages of that Book. 'The created universe is waiting with eager expectation for God's sons to be revealed', wrote Paul, and, a few sentences further on: 'Up to the present, as we know, the whole created universe in all its parts groans as if in the pangs of childbirth' (*Romans 8:19, 22*). Put all that together and it is saying: God creates, but creation is in a state of incompleteness, waiting for the response of people who are in tune with the Will of God, waiting for the day when creation is renewed and completed.

What do we really mean when we speak of God as the Creator? That is not a question seeking an answer in technical terms – that is the job of the scientist. It is unhelpful to take the Genesis story literally. It is a poem, not a scientific treatise. There is no need to try and set it over against the theory of evolution and the modern discoveries of natural laws. The so-called 'creationists' think they have to fight against all this. They don't. I myself am a 'creationist' in the sense that I believe God is the Author of all that is; but I respect and accept the findings of geologists, biologists and anthropologists. They are exploring origins. The aim of religion is to explore meanings. There need be no hostility between the two explorers. It is like exploring a piece of music, say a Beethoven symphony. Those concerned with the theory of music will explore its notation, point and counterpoint, the mathematics of its notation and harmonies. But there is another way of discovering Beethoven – and that is listening to the music and feeling what he is saying in terms of emotional uplift and meaning. To speak about the 'creation of the universe' is to listen to what its music is saying.

And what does it say? It says there is a purpose in the universe; 'In the beginning, God . . .' That purpose, it says, is a loving purpose; 'God saw that it was good'. True, problems remain; is the earthquake that kills thousands 'good'? Is cancer 'good'? Certainly, 'the whole creation groans'. And this suggests that the creative process is a continuing one. What is more, we humans are called upon to help in that continuing process, e.g., to do research on the causes and cure of cancer. God, we believe, created humans in his image; and that implies we are made to share in his creative purpose; 'God blessed them and said: "Be fruitful and increase; fill the earth and subdue it." ' (Though this has been wrongly understood widely as 'exploit it'.)

Our partnership with God

And so our attention is directed sharply to the partnership of humans with God in creation. In the second creation story (*Genesis: 2*) this is made clear: ' . . . When the Lord God made the earth and the heavens, there was neither shrub nor plant growing on the earth because the Lord God had sent no rain, nor was there anyone to till the ground' (*Genesis 2:4–5*). So (to switch to Paul) he was 'waiting for the sons of God to be revealed'. All this should help us to a more sophisticated understanding. We can say that God created because he is Love and waited for those who would respond to his love in obedience to his call. Creation is loving and response to loving. 'Without God,' said Augustine, 'man cannot; without man, God will not.' And the beauty and the bounty of our world is manifestly the result of this partnership.

I like what was written by the historian, G. M. Trevelyan, about what most of us would agree is one of the most beautiful parts of Britain, the Lake District: 'It was only in the course of the eighteenth century that the beauty of Wordsworth's homeland attained the moment of rightful balance between nature and man. In previous centuries the valleys were choked, tangled, empty and featureless.'[4] It is as if God deliberately left his world half-finished, waiting for man to complete it. That goes for everything in our experience. God gave us children; but we 'produce' them and bring them up. As Eve rather nicely put it when she gave birth to Cain: 'With the help of the Lord I have brought into being a male child (*Genesis 4:1*). Pause for thought here. She seemed to think she'd done the main job – the Lord just helping a bit! (Poor old Adam doesn't seem to come into the process at all!)

But maybe here we can put our finger on an important point. We are indeed God's partners – but we are *junior* partners. When we forget that then the trouble begins. The Genesis story didn't overlook that; in the garden was the 'tree of the knowledge of good and evil'; if they ate of that they were doomed to die. Don't think of this tree as meaning our knowing the difference between right and wrong. The 'tree' stands for what are the ultimate values and what are not; and that is God's ultimate law, not ours. To 'eat of that tree' is an attempt to make our own evaluation of what constitutes 'good' and what 'bad'; in short, it is to try to *be God*. That is when the partnership goes bad on us.

This concept of partnership with God in creation needs to be spelt out in more detail; otherwise we may speak of it too easily without seeing its implications. 'Partnership with God' can remain just a theoretical theological phrase unless we try to express it in real, this-worldly terms. It involves other forms of partnership, without which partnership with God is emptied of all meaning.

Partnership with Nature and our fellows

We tend sometimes to smile when we hear of gardeners who talk to their plants and flowers, but there is something important and meaningful here. There has to be an understanding of, a sympathy with, an acceptance of Nature and its ways. In short, there has to be a partnership with Nature. It is as necessary to ask, 'what is the natural world saying and striving towards?' as to decide what we want to do to shape and direct and discipline it. It isn't any good telling a rosebush to produce carrots! It is no good 'telling' a forest that its trees are only there so that we can cut them down to make planks for ships or paper for newspapers. If we do, then the forest and its environment will respond in protest by producing a waterless desert. Partnership with Nature means respect for it, discovering and going along with its laws, not trying to impose our selfish desires on it. The Prophets of the Old Testament were alert to this. Said Jeremiah to the people of Judah: 'Your wrongdoing has upset nature's order, and your sins have kept away her bounty' (*Jeremiah 5:25*).

Partnership with God in creation also involves partnership with all other members of the human family. It means sharing, it means remembering their needs as well as our own. The deforestation and resultant drought and starvation for the local human inhabitants of an area is a direct result of men forgetting this practical application of our work in the creative process. Even in a country like England, where the commercial will of the rich and powerful is making nature fulfil their desires, we see the direct result in the ever-deepening gulf between the comfortable inhabitants of suburbia and the horror of the inner-city slum dwellers. Do not talk easily about our being in 'partnership with God' if that doesn't in practice mean partnership with nature and your fellows.

What we are seeing today is, in many ways, a clear demonstration of what I have just written. The greed of men has led them to subject the natural world to their own self-centred ambitions. The results: pollution of water and air, piles of rubbish in well-off societies and millions of near-starving people in poverty-stricken societies. So often the unspoken sentiment seems to be: 'Take what you want and the devil take the hindmost!' It is not enough for Christian people to join the general grumble; we have, by word and deed, to demand that God's law to love your neighbour should be taken seriously. In a society where getting rich quick, and idolising material possessions and one's own personal comfort are the main guidelines of living, of course creation goes wrong. This is why 'the whole creation groans, waiting for the sons of God to be revealed'.

What can I do?

In what ways are we – as individuals – living a way of life which is consistent with being 'the sons of God'? In what ways is mankind facing its creative responsibilities. All is not gloom and doom. There is a growing sense of mutual responsibility; there is an immense reservoir of compassion for the suffering, which comes to light when appeals are made on television and radio for the victims of disasters (e.g. the starving in parts of Africa) and people give money with great generosity. Sadly, however, the militaristic ambitions of those in power, or who covet power, make the conditions of the afflicted worse. And the ambitions of the technologically advanced north of our planet only increase the bad conditions of the south. But there are many protests and movements for alleviation. Again, the great benefits for all of us arising from the patient researches of medical scientists, the care displayed by nurses and doctors, the churches (like the Methodist Church involved in 'Mission alongside the Poor') – all these are hopeful signs that our partnership with God in creation is being taken seriously. I even heard a woman who is a supporter of the Green Party urging us now to speak of God as 'green'!

So we wrestle with the problems of ecology. There *is* hope. The creation 'groans' indeed, but as Paul suggested, it is the groan of childbirth, not of death-pangs. In our own individual lives, the habits we have, the life-style we adopt are important; we have our part to play. There is something every man, every woman can do to share in creative partnership with God. In 1983 the Vancouver Assembly of the World Council of Churches invited churches to engage 'in a conciliar process of mutual commitment to justice, peace and the integrity of creation'. One result was a great assembly in Basel in Switzerland in 1989 of representatives of all the churches in Europe. They discussed these matters and issued a *Message* to be followed up by local churches everywhere. Their message spoke of the evil of war, poverty and hunger, and the necessity for all to be able to share the earth's resources. It stated:

> We do not have unlimited freedom to exploit nature. We reject all threats to life and all waste of resources and energy.

Its Statement ended with this prayer:

> Lord, make us instruments of your justice;
> Make us instruments of your peace;
> Make us instruments for the renewal of your creation.

The World Council of Churches has also made this statement:

> We affirm in word and deed God's sovereignty over all creation, and pray for the establishment of God's promised *shalom*. We are stewards of creation; we seek a just sharing of the land; we aim to be peacemakers; we probe the relationship between earth and human culture.

And a prayer from the Conference of Methodists for World Mission in 1989:

> We remember with penitence the continuing pollution and destruction of our God-given environment by our industries and lifestyle. We remember with hope our daily opportunities to make choices to live more simply, to be better stewards of creation.

References

1. Genesis, Chapter 1.
2. Revelation 21:1.
3. Genesis 1:28.
4. G. M. Trevelyan (1944) *Illustrated English Social History,* **Vol 3**, p. 10. Longmans, Green & Company. London.
5. *A New Dictionary of Christian Theology* (1983). Ed by Alan Richardson and John Bowden. SCM Press Ltd. London.

Questions for Discussion

1. What insights into the partnership of humans with God in the work of creation do the opening chapters of Genesis give us? Do the healing miracles of Jesus add to these insights?
2. What difference to your understanding of the purpose of living does it make to be able to affirm: 'God is the Creator'?
3. It is suggested in this chapter that creation is 'incomplete'. Is this to cast doubt on God's creative power? If not, what does it add to our understanding of the *wonder* of God as Creator?
4. An article in '*A New Dictionary of Christian Theology*'[5] says that Christian thinkers have failed to contribute significantly to current debates on ecology, conservation and the uses of technology. Do you think this is so, and if so, why?

9. Sharers in Life and Death

Our responsibility

If we are called to a partnership with God in developing the world, we are certainly called to partner him in peopling the world. The word used for this particular form of creative partnership speaks for itself – procreation. Our age is different from any that has preceded it in that the work of sharing with God in the production of human lives is seen to be our responsibility. In the past the birth of children has been seen as God's activity, with men and women having little to say in the matter. But now we are starkly aware of the problem of over-population, of the wretched poverty and near-starvation of large numbers of people in some countries, such as Africa and India; and we have the mechanical means of regulating births.

We have at last awakened to the fact that not every birth is a 'gift of God', that upon our shoulders has been placed the responsibility for determining when and how many human lives should be created. A modern western man and his wife will (unless deterred by 'religious' or medical reasons) decide when they will have children, and how many. Along with this has come a deeper understanding of the fact that sexual love is not only a means to the birth of a child; that part of its creative power lies in its making a bond between a man and a woman of infinite joy and strength. Thus the comment that the only legitimate form of birth-control is to refrain from sexual intercourse is seen as a narrowing down of the purpose of such intercourse to something less than God's intention for the joyous fulfilment of his children.

All forms of birth control, it would seem, are legitimate and part of God's offer of partnership in the creative process. This, obviously, is a debatable point so I can only state my own point of view here. Of course, the use of contraceptives *may* be for purely selfish purposes, just as man's dominion over other parts of the created world may be misused. But used with a sense of responsibility they can add to the joy, peace and contentment of the human race. A 1962 British Council of Churches publication, had a helpful comment to make on the whole question:

> This issue of world population raises in an obvious form the particular question we are now considering – how much is man called upon to be an active and deciding fellow-worker with God? Few Christians appear to doubt that they are called to use their minds, allied to instruments and drugs, to combat disease, alleviate pain and prolong life, but some oppose vehemently the use of human judgement allied to mechanical and chemical means to prevent conception. It is in fact the combination of victory over terrible death-rates with still unrestricted birth-rates which presents us with our problem. Man today has gained an immense measure of control over disease in comparison with past generations. He has also now the power by mechanical or chemical means to control the number of births. Is this a power which invades the sphere which should be reserved for God's sole action? To this question the Anglican and the great majority of Protestant churches now answer firmly, 'No'.[1]

Abortion

This new responsibility upon man leads to a further and more controversial aspect of the matter. It would seem a logical next step that there may be occasions when it would be right for a foetus to be aborted, and to speak of such occasions as 'murder' would be an exaggeration. All life comes from God, every human life is a part of God, becoming independent within a physical frame in order that it may grow to become a personality free to return to God in conscious communion. But does this outlaw abortion? The controversy on this matter rages fiercely at the present time. The question upon which a decision must be made concerning the rightness or wrongness of abortion is this: is abortion simply a form of infanticide? Is it in fact the murder of a child, only at an earlier stage than was commonly practised by some cultures in ancient times – within the womb instead of outside it? If the answer is 'Yes' then there can be no further argument; abortion is murder and to be abhorred as violently as civilised men abhor infanticide. But is the answer 'yes'? Can the few-days-old foetus be regarded as independent and conscious in any real sense?

It is at this point that the disagreement between the anti-abortionists and others comes to a sharp focus. The anti-abortionist declares that a new human life begins at the moment of conception. Others would admit that the foetus is 'alive', but would ask: 'can a few-days-old foetus be regarded as independent and conscious in any meaningful sense?' This question has brought forth conflicting responses from sincere Christians. In introducing a Report of 'The Status of the Unborn Child' Professor Ian Leck said that no hard and fast rules could be laid down here: 'We affirm that for resolving such conflicts between the rights of different members of the human community we have not been given any rules. Those concerned with the unborn human must, therefore, be allowed to make their own individual decisions. What we can do and what we must do is to provide the basis for such decision-making, to affirm above all that love must guide our decision-making since God is love.'[2] He stressed the Report's affirmation that from conception onwards the unborn is human and a part of the human community. The unborn was an object of God's love and a bearer of his image. But the Report did not therefore conclude that the unborn had an absolute right to life and therefore did not totally rule out experiments on the under-14-days-old pre-embryo and neither did it rule out all abortion. He gave reasons for the Report's conclusions; the unborn was not a meaningfully recognisable human individual until two weeks after conception when the embryo begins to form from the ball of cells the pre-embryo has by this time become. Then many, probably most, miscarry in the course of nature and this was hard to square with the view that they had an absolute right to life.

Nevertheless the question which those who do not accept the

anti-abortionist position must ask with the utmost seriousness is this: Have we any right to interfere with the creative process whereby that foetus is now on the way to becoming a full human being? This question has to be in the forefront of the thinking of any who are considering aborting a foetus. There are no reasons to proceed except two: the prospective mother's life is in danger or the life of the child to be born is in equal danger. Abortion as something freely available to meet people's self-centred requirements or to rid them of responsibilities is wrong. Yet I believe it can be argued that there may be compassion, when circumstances threaten the child-to-be with wretchedness for years to come, in giving that life back to God to whom it belongs until such time as a needed and wanted body is ready for its earthly life. I am aware that to write in this way in a few words does no justice to a very difficult and emotive subject. The one point I am making is that God truly seems to have given men and women the responsibility of peopling the earth and deciding the right conditions in which a child should be born.

Genetic technology

There are further questions that come from medical science's advances in genetic research and technology: fertilisation produced artificially, even outside the womb of the mother-to-be; the ability to determine to some extent the work of the genes – the sex of the child and the type of mind that will develop. Baffling questions indeed – still in their infancy, still to be tackled in depth. We cannot evade them. But any answers we try to find must at all times bear in mind our 'junior' partnership with God – even as we have to bear this in mind in our use of nuclear energy. As with the wrong use of nuclear power, so with the wrong use of genetic knowledge, we may be on the way to the destruction of the human race.

It might seem illogical to suggest that genetic engineering or abortion might be leading to the destruction of the human race. Their aim is, for many, after all, the praiseworthy one of avoiding the birth of an incomplete or damaged human being. But is it sound logic to argue that unless every human is physically and mentally 'perfect', the world of human relationships is somehow impoverished? It was part of the Nazi ideology to produce a pure Aryan race by getting rid of all who did not attain their ideal – a 'policy' which led to the killing of the aged and infirm. Was this not, at the same time, the killing of human compassion, caring, sharing of courage and indeed victory through shared suffering?

I think again of my experience in the village of Papworth where in that community of disabled people there was more joy and laughter and companionship and hope than is usually to be found in those well-off, thoroughly healthy suburbs where such disabilities are rare. There is a place in our experience for acceptance of what nature has determined. (Is this, perhaps, the basic message of the book of Job?) I realise the anguish of parents who have to face the problem, say, of their few-days-old child who is gravely ill and whether to let the child die or not. But I shrink from the thought that the day may come when it is the accepted thing always to 'kill' such a child.

Euthanasia and the Hospice Movement

The responsibility of our partnership with God in the realm of human life leads us into even stranger and more difficult areas. If we now find that we have the right and duty to determine when a child shall be born, what about the other end of the spectrum of life – the decision about when a person should die? Have we the right – within properly agreed limitations (e.g. when a person suffers from a terminal illness or has been born hideously handicapped) – to end life? The debate on euthanasia continues as vigorously as that on abortion. 'Thou shalt not kill' is the clinching argument for some, but not for others who are equally, sometimes more, compassionate and responsible in their thinking. If creating is loving, may there not be cases in which the most creative thing of all would be to destroy – as we put an animal out of its misery? There is, I admit, as yet no clear understanding in my own mind about what is 'right' in this matter. Certainly the right to regulate births does not automatically give the right to regulate deaths, for in the one case we are not obviously interfering in the fate of a living person; in the other we are. I confess that, for me, euthanasia is not yet part of our duty in our partnership with God, though the easing of pain and the making of death an easier passage to eternity certainly is.

Here it seems relevant to write about the hospice movement which might offer an alternative to so-called 'mercy-killing'. The name of Cecily Saunders is important here. Trained as a nurse and a doctor, she felt the call to concentrate on care for the dying, to explore ways to ease pain so that the lot of the terminally ill could be one of meaning, fullness, even of joy, rather than of despair. She gained experience from, and contributed a great deal to, the work of St Joseph's Hospice in Hackney in East London (run by the Roman Catholic Sisters of Charity), and in due course founded St Christopher's Hospice in Sydenham. Today there is an increasing number of hospices, many attached to established hospitals. I add my own testimony. When I was a minister in Hackney I was a Free Church Chaplain to St Joseph's Hospice and always felt uplifted by the positive and joyous atmosphere of the place – its staff and its patients. Where once the terminally ill lay doped because of their pain, and inert, today many of them are alert and indeed contributing positively to the community. Cecily Saunders said that in 1961 she took the chairman of the Voluntary Euthanasia Society round St Joseph's and he wrote to her: 'I feel that there would be little or no problem of euthanasia if all the terminal diseased folk could end their lives in that atmosphere you have done so much to create – but alas, that can hardly be for many a long year.' Since then, of course, many more hospices have come into existence. In such an atmosphere euthanasia seems to fade away as a fairly meaningless option. The very process of dying is 'swallowed up in victory' and made a meaningful part of human pilgrimage.

The debate continues – in all serious minds. A publication by the Church Information Office, *On Dying Well*,[3] makes a valuable contribution. Whilst its conclusion is that there should be no change in the law to permit euthanasia because of grave dangers that might result – such as patients being put under pressure to allow themselves to be put away – the Report has this positive thing to say:

> In its narrow current sense, euthanasia implies killing, and it is misleading to extend it to cover decisions not to preserve life by artificial means when it would be better for the patient to be

> allowed to die. Such decisions, coupled with a determination to give the patient as good a death as possible, may be quite legitimate. Nor should it be used to cover the giving of drugs for the relief of pain and other distress in cases where there is a risk that they may marginally shorten the patient's life. This, too, we think legitimate.

That strikes me as creative thinking and offers a positive suggestion as to the kind of partnership we can share with God even in the solemn realm of death.

Thus, the work of the scientist, the technologist, the medical doctor, and the responsible parent is all part of the partnership of human beings with God in the continuing creative process, and we cannot evade the deep and complex questions which it lays upon us.

References

1. *Human Reproduction – a study of some emergent problems and questions in the Light of the Christian Faith (1962).* Council of Churches for Britain and Ireland. London.
2. Ian Leck (1990), *The Status of the Unborn Child.* Introduced during the 1990 Methodist Conference.
3. *On Dying Well* (1975), Church Information Office, Church House Publishing, London.

Questions for Discussion

1. What are your views on the rightness or wrongness of abortion? If it is permissible, what conditions and safeguards must be observed?
2. Is euthanasia ('mercy-killing') ever justifiable? What are the inherent dangers in legalising it?
3. Do you consider that today the very idea of euthanasia should be dispensed with?

10. Growing Old Gracefully

Continuing to live into old age is the prospect for more people in our country today than ever before. It has been estimated that by the year 2000 a tenth of the world's population will be aged over 60. In the UK there are more than three million people over 75, with a rapid increase expected over the next decade. This constitutes a problem for society – both financially and in making adequate accommodation for those needing special care.

The needs of older people

More especially, old age brings its problems for the old themselves.

Declining health is one. Not that this is inevitable; modern medical knowledge means that many of the sicknesses that once incapacitated or quickly killed the old can now be dealt with or eradicated.

Inactivity is another – in the sense that the time of retirement from regular and meaningful work has now arrived, so that many feel there is no longer any real purpose in their lives; each day brings increasing boredom – or the prospect of just sitting and looking at TV.

Loneliness is another. This can come about because of the concept of what constitutes a family being narrower in our country than in, for example, some African countries. A man and woman marry and look for a small house for them and their hoped-for children to live in. There is little enough room for them – let alone ageing parents. Consequently ageing parents often live alone (and this is what they frequently want anyway) or in expensive and sometimes unpleasant nursing-homes or Old People's homes or the geriatric wards of hospitals. (I shall say more about this aspect of old people's aloneness later.)

Loss of friends by death is another. 'I have more friends in the next world than in this one', said an old person to me with a rueful smile. This sense of the number of one's friends gradually diminishing comes sharply to mind for the elderly when the time comes to write the annual Christmas cards and the recognition that several on last year's list must now be crossed out; they are no longer at an address that can be reached by a Christmas card.

In the light of all the above, I suggest that the ageing have three basic needs – Security, Status, Activity.

Security

When the old live happily with their children, this can be good. But not necessarily so. Geoffrey Gorer, the sociologist, was of the opinion that the problem of old people was not to be solved by urging that all young people should have their older folk living with them. He was wont to remind people of Aneurin Bevan's words about old people clinging to their privacy: they do not want to be dependent on others. But the time may come when their love of independence becomes a danger; arthritic problems, for example, make them unsteady on their feet; a fall in the middle of the night when they go to the toilet may leave them lying cold and helpless for many hours. The frail elderly must have regular visits from friends, fellow church-members, social workers, health visitors, home-helps. And an essential piece of equipment is a pendant worn round the neck – a Link Alarm – whereby the owner of it may at any time get a message to the controller of it who will immediately arrange assistance to be sent. In time, living on one's own may become a practical impossibility.

Proper provision of basic needs is required. The financial angle of this must not be overlooked. An old friend of mine once wrote for me a list of 'the fears of old age'. Among them was what he called 'Fear of poverty or lessening of spending power'. The Old Age Pension is good – though not good enough. Old people also have the right to certain extra allowances to ensure they shall not live below a certain financial level. But do many old people know what these rights are? And if they do, does pride make them shudder at the very words 'Social Security'? It smacks to them of charity, of their being classed as 'paupers'. It must be brought home to them that this is not so. These are their rights, the money is their due as surely as that paid by government in respect of the children in a family. Younger people must do all they can to go into these matters with old people, and encourage them to get rid of their prejudices and mistaken pride.

But when old people are no longer able to live in independent houses of their own, it is urgent that decent homes be found for them – homes where they will still have independence together with some kind of oversight in case they are ill. How we should support the work of such organisations as *Help the Aged, Age Concern* and the *Centre for Policy on Ageing*, one of whose aims is to press society and government to ensure that such homes are available. A great contribution has been made to this by the churches. The *Methodist Homes for the Aged* (MHA) is one example. Each resident has his or her own room – a living-room equipped with the person's own furniture. Privacy is assured whilst meals are normally taken together, so that there is fellowship. The local Methodist Church has a 'Home Committee' and its job is to organise concerts, socials and parties.

At the Home where I have been the chaplain a regular Sunday evening service is held in the lounge. The Home is named among the other churches on the Circuit Plan and preachers are appointed in the same way as in the other churches in the circuit. The MHA leaflet, *'Putting new life into old age'*, after describing the needs of the old and the physical ways in which MHA tries to meet them, continues: 'Over and above all the caring that we provide, we bring love, down-to-earth, practical, Christian love. We encourage our old people to be themselves, to enjoy life, to flower again. We help to make their physical problems more bearable, to find their own resources of strength, to learn how to cope with each day in its own way, and to look forward with renewed spirit to tomorrow. This is the philosophy of MHA: to increase the capacity for living among the elderly in our care – to put new life into their old age, to provide fulfilment.'[1]

Let me mention also the increasing number of *Abbeyfield Old People's Homes* – ordinary properties, many of them, bought and adapted into flats where each old person has his or her own entirely private room, and the care of a trained matron. There are the *Salvation Army Eventide Homes* and *Church Army Housing Ltd.*, to mention but two other such organisations. But some of the government and private homes show no such care and instead of the joy one nearly always finds in those Homes named above, there is an atmosphere of helplessness, of nothingness, of sitting round in a circle with nothing to do but watch the everlasting telly! It is a true calling to work in a Home for the Aged – and I salute the many I have met for whom it is just that.

Status

Most of us would vigorously deny that we regard old people as unimportant; yet so much of our actual behaviour gives that impression. And the old feel it; they feel forgotten. And you are forgotten when you do not appear to the community to be important enough to be given time and attention.

How much we have to learn here from the Jews. The Hebrews had a tremendous respect for age. Their Law said: 'Rise in the presence of grey hairs, give honour to the aged . . .' (*Leviticus 19:32*). And it was not sentimental kindness that led to that respect. It was a realisation that old people have something to give that younger people just do not – cannot – yet possess and without which the life of the community is all the poorer. The writer of Proverbs saw that the young have something to contribute and the old have something to contribute – each distinctive – to the fullness of a community's happiness: 'The glory of young men is their strength, the dignity of old men their grey hairs' (*Proverbs 20:29*). It isn't that 'grey hair' has some mystical significance in itself. It is rather that the old can have a wisdom which is the result of a cumulative process of studying, discovery and experience. In a deep sense, only the more aged can claim it. It comes only after a long life – rightly lived. It is not always the case! Some old people can get self-centred, negatively critical of change. But age and youth are complementary to each other. The Bible is full of the exploits of young men; but nearly always behind them is some wise old person able to interpret to the young the call of God which they would have missed otherwise. Eli interpreted God's call to the young Samuel. Samuel when old was the agent of God's call to David. The aged Simeon interpreted to the young parents of the child Jesus what was to be his destiny. The ageing Paul put young Timothy on the right lines. And we may add here that the vigorous John Wesley looked continuously to his old mother, Susanna, for guidance as his Methodist revival gained momentum.

It is disturbing to see the increasing segregation of the ages in our time. I am not suggesting that we should return to those days when the young had to keep their mouths shut and accept as the truth all the words that the old spoke. I am suggesting that we should see afresh that to be rich, human life must consist of the ideas and work of the young, aided and considered by the old. By visiting the old, being willing to listen to them, discuss problems with them, and open our hearts to them – that is for our own good, and it is to restore to them the status they have so unjustly lost.

Activity

What can old people do with their declining years? My old friend put down on his list of fears: 'Fear of being useless'. He added that he would urge the old to get part-time jobs. 'Get a morning job', he wrote, 'at a petrol station, delivering the papers – anything!' Could more commercial firms provide such jobs, even train the retired for them?

There comes the time when regular work is out of the question. Then what? Thank God for old people's social clubs – and those who run them. In such clubs the old can do so much themselves – in choirs, concert parties. They can be encouraged to take up extra skills – painting, music. The sociologist mentioned earlier wrote: 'There is no reason why the period of retirement should not be regarded in a positive and constructive way, as a time when many interests and activities, for which there has been neither time nor opportunity earlier, can now be undertaken. There are some colleges offering courses in various subjects – music, painting, philosophy – for old people, and these courses are well-attended and keenly pursued. The idea that retirement is just a period of decrepitude during which one waits for the last journey to the graveyard is an idea we should do away with.' Death will come, but as it draws near the old can say, if they have insisted on activity and thought, what the old man Simeon said when he had spoken to Mary and Joseph: 'Now, Lord, you are releasing your servant in peace, according to your promise. For I have seen with my own eyes the deliverance you have made ready in full view of all nations' (*Luke 2:29–31*).

The Christian approach to growing older

We end this chapter by examining what is the basic biblical approach to the process of growing older. I discern two elements:

(1) *The Bible sees the secret of life – long serenity in rooting one's life in that which is changeless and eternal.* We have to sit loosely to the things that belong to this world, recognising that they are transient. The writer of *Psalm 39:4, 5* says: 'Lord, let me know my end, and the number of my days; tell me how short my Life is to be. I know you have made my days a mere span long, and my whole life is as nothing in your sight. A human being, however firm he stands, is but a puff of wind.' That sounds rather pessimistic, but there is something healthy in this attitude, because it accords with fact – healthy because it lifts the purpose of our life out of the temporal and sets it in the context of the eternal. If we are made for eternal life, then the events of our 70 or 80 years here are a small part indeed of the sum total of existence and must be seen in their right perspective.

This does not mean that we are to withdraw from our present world. We can work hard, play hard, enjoy to the full the various experiences that God has provided; but we will not set a final value on them because they do not have a final value. There is a hymn I used to dislike singing, especially the last verse: 'Nothing on earth do I desire but Thy pure love within my breast'; I disliked it because there is so much I *do* desire! I desire to retain good health; I desire certain persons or things.

But in recent years I have come to see the wisdom of the hymn. To desire is to long to retain for ever and to centre all one's energies on that which is desired. But what lasting satisfaction can be found in such a desire for things which are bound to change or pass away in the course of the years? The man who has set his whole desire on physical fitness – made a god of athletic prowess – is going to be sadly disillusioned when inevitably his muscles become less flexible. The woman who has centred her whole desire on being physically attractive will begin to watch her mirror (like the queen in *Snow White*) with increasing anxiety for signs of grey hairs and lines at the corners of her eyes. Even to desire a person in this way is an illusion, for death will one day step in. You may love and enjoy these things, but anything more is to worship them and you cannot worship the transient. It is because we so often trust the transient as if it were permanent that the process of growing older can be so agonising, leaving us feeling for ever insecure. Only the person who has anchored his or her life in that which is changeless will be able to go an even way, unafraid and at peace.

All this is not something to be brought just to the notice of the old – but, perhaps, more importantly, to the young. 'Remember your Creator in the days of your youth . . .' Think of God while you are young, says (*Ecclesiastes 12:1*), lest you find you cannot have any sense of His reality when you are old. The secret of passing through life's successive stages without fear, disillusion or a sense of becoming a 'backnumber' is to be rooted in the everlasting love of God. Paul wrote: '. . . Our eyes are fixed, not on the things that are seen, but on the things that are unseen, for what is seen is transient, what is unseen is eternal' (*2 Corinthians 4:18*). Here is a prayer from *Compline* – the final service of the day in many Anglican Churches; it is an evening prayer, but with the slight adjustment of a word or two applies to any hour of the day, any day of the year, any year of our life:

> Protect us, O Lord, through the silent hours of this night, that we, who are fatigued by the chances and changes of this fleeting world, may repose upon your eternal changelessness.

(2) *The Bible sees the whole of a person's life, from birth to death, as a continuous progress to maturity.* If you asked people to draw a graph indicating the course of life's happiness, many would draw a line that began low, rose to a high point representing the ages between 20 and 40 and then began to descend. You see why. In youth you have your full physical powers; you have a multiplicity of interests – even ideals; there seems no end to the possibilities opening out before you. But with the coming of the older years, physical powers decay to some extent, ideals are modified to fit realities; life becomes narrowed down to fewer activities – your job, home responsibilities, limitations set by economic circumstances. So middle age is in danger of becoming a time of monotony, narrowed horizons, dreams shattered. The climax of life is past; the rest is decline.

This will not be so for those who are grasping the Christian understanding of life. They see each stage in life as something not complete in itself but to be enjoyed and then left behind as they pass on to the next. Each phase they see as a time for learning something which can be carried with them to the next phase. Thus: the trust and simplicity of childhood they will take with them into adulthood, but they will leave behind childish habits and practices; they have outgrown them. The idealism and zest of youth they will take into their full adulthood, but they'll leave behind the irresponsibility of that period. The poise and dignity of adulthood they will take with them into old age, but they'll not try to hold on to the power they wielded when they were in positions of authority.

So at every stage they will pick up and retain some fresh quality that builds their spirit, always looking forward. Thus they will grow increasingly mature and life will offer ever wider vistas of wonder. There need be no period of decline. Change – yes; differences of emphasis – yes; but no decline. The trouble is that so many do not want to grow up. J. A. Hadfield, a well-known psychologist in the 1930s, said that the primary condition of mental health is to advance with every stage of life, retaining what is good and lasting of the old but advancing to the new. Those who strive, he said, to remain 'young' merely succeed in becoming stale and fossilised – and a fossil is the petrified remains of a dead thing. He said,

'The secret of perpetual youth is to grow old.' We are reminded of Browning's poem:

> Grow old along with me, the best is yet to be;
> the last of life for which the first was planned.
> Our times are in his hands, who saith: 'A whole I planned'.
> Youth shows but half; trust God, see all nor be afraid.

Herein is the Christian meaning of 'growing old gracefully'; it is growing by the grace of God; this grace, which is God's gift to us, prepares for us 'an eternal weight of glory beyond all comparison'. In Him past, present and future coexist. We are with Him always, yet grow nearer to Him every day. Eternal life is both our future hope and our daily experience. That is the measure of God's grace – and in that grace we grow.

References

1. *Putting Life into Old Age* (1984), The Methodist Homes for the Aged, Epworth House, Derby.

Questions for Discussion

1. What do older members of the group consider are the benefits of growing older?
2. How can the gifts of old and young people be shared to the mutual benefit of both?

11. A Violent Age

It is often said that we live in a violent age. Our attention is directed to statistics which tell of increased crimes, many of them violent and resulting in deaths; attacks on the elderly in their homes; parental abuse of children; fighting of a vicious sort between football fans; unruly teenage gangs; drug-abuse; the hijacking of aircraft. Many people are consequently afraid to go out of doors after dark or walk in once-peaceful parks and open spaces. The impression is given that we have become an uncaring society, that we're no longer good neighbours but rather aggressive individuals or groups, with an accepted initial approach to our fellows of suspicious unfriendliness. What, we may ask, has gone wrong?

Are we really more violent than previous ages?

Before passing judgement too hastily we should remember that violence has been a common factor throughout the centuries. Read Dickens and see! In Victorian times the police often had to go about in pairs in much of London's East End; it was the only safe way to patrol the streets; children were left on the streets without food, without shoes. And what about the highwaymen of earlier times who made all travel precarious? In some ways we are a far more caring society now, as is shown by the generous response of the public to appeals on television to help children in need or the starving in Africa. Generally speaking, it is safe to travel on the roads, and we all have access to the social and medical services. This, too, is a welcome aspect of modern society. Perhaps the violence of our time seems worse because instances of it are brought to our immediate notice through the media (especially TV) and this was not possible 50 years ago.

Nevertheless, today's violence is a reality and it is necessary to ask what are the causes of its apparent increase in intensity. But before doing that we need to examine what we mean by 'violence'. What are its roots and to what extent is it a natural and necessary element in our human nature?

A right kind of aggression

Within all living creatures there is an energy, a driving-force that is needed if life – that of individuals and of the human race itself – is to develop and survive. This driving-force takes various forms; some seem positive, some negative; some life-creating, some life-destroying. If I want to make my garden more beautiful and productive I must put both forms of energy into my work in it: destructive in that I try to destroy weeds and creatures which hinder growth; creative in that I water the plants and try to increase the value of the soil. This cannot be described as violence, even though it sometimes takes the form of an attack. It could be called aggressiveness – necessary acts of aggression. It is the use of force. In his book, *The Violence Inside*, Paul Tournier writes: 'We must acknowledge that there is in nature – whether we call it aggression or violence – a force which is normal and healthy, which introduces a relationship of rivalry between individuals, a dynamic equilibrium which can be observed in all vital phenomena. It is more than an effect of life; it is the very essence of life.'[1] A growing child is encouraged to release and make use of this aggressiveness; he must attack ignorance, and struggle to learn to talk and read and write and become an independent individual. That is using force. A parent will not hesitate to use force to stop his child from suddenly running into a busy street.

Turning to the Bible, we should observe that the basic teaching of Jesus and Paul often seems to be more the offer of a life of conflict than a life of peace. 'You must not think', said Jesus, 'that I have come to bring peace to the earth; I have not come to bring peace but a sword' (*Matthew 10:34*). And his actions confirmed his words – the cleansing of the temple, his denunciation in hard words of some of the Pharisees' actions, the casting out of demons. He seemed to be saying that the truly fulfilled life was a constant battle. He did not teach non-resistance to evil. So with Paul: 'We are not contending against flesh and blood, but against the principalities, against the powers, against the world-rulers of this present darkness, against the spiritual hosts of wickedness in the heavenly places' (*Ephesians 6:12*). There is a war on – a war against sin, against all that cuts humans off from God.

But there is another side to the teaching of Jesus and Paul. Jesus said: '. . . Do not resist those who wrong you. If anyone slaps you on the right cheek, turn and offer him the other also . . . Love your enemies and pray for your persecutors' (*Matthew 5:39, 44*). Paul said: 'Must Christian go to law with Christian – and before unbelievers at that? . . . Indeed, you suffer defeat by going to law with one another at all. Why not rather submit to wrong: Why not let yourself be defrauded?' (*1 Corinthians 6:6–7*). The apparent contradiction between the two sets of quotes here given are resolved in this way: the first are calls to destroy evil; the second are calls to refuse to destroy your fellows. It is when the rightful aggressive force in a person – done in the cause of love – is turned into a force done in the cause of lovelessness that it becomes violence. We may indeed say that all sins are the perversions of right instincts. Violence is the corruption of the fight for life in which we are all involved.

The causes of violence today

If our society has indeed become more violent, we must seek the reasons. I would suggest that these reasons can be discussed under the following three headings:

(1) *The loss of a sense of the importance of human relationships.* This is often shown in the weakening of family ties. True, there is a danger that family relationships might become so close that people are cut off from awareness of the wider family of humanity. This danger is reflected in a too-strong love for one's own nation or race to the exclusion of others. Yet to

belong to a family in which the love of parents for the children and of the children for the parents and brothers and sisters is real and deep is to possess a sense of worth and security and meaning that removes all feelings of loneliness and rejection that can come upon those denied any real family experience. When a family breaks up, and in one-parent families, such feelings are a real danger. Without a father a child is denied a power to cope with living which maybe only a male parent can fully give. Without a mother a child is denied that sense of physical and mental belonging that only a mother's closeness (which began in the womb) can offer. The breakdown of so much family life today has led young teenagers to feel unwanted, driven them away to the streets, to homelessness, to the often fruitless task of searching for a substitute family by joining a gang, angry with a society which is denying them their natural rights.

(2) *The hidden violence of an unjust society*. There is one factor in the total situation which is not always realised, namely that the violence of so many young people may be a reaction to a violence directed at them, though hidden and not recognised – the disguised violence of an unjust society's treatment of them. It may not seem a proper use of the word 'violence' to describe some of the injustices they suffer thus. Yet the huge disproportion between the situation of the wealthy and the poverty-stricken, between the opportunities given to those who have had the good fortune of a good upbringing – school, college, good prospects of a job – and the deprivation of those whose background denies them these privileges, is clear. Is this not like a barrier to the deprived ones, stating, 'This is not for you; keep out; don't get in our way' – a barrier which is equivalent to a violent rebuff? There may be no killing or physical force but it is a forced limitation of the offer of life in all its fullness as hurtful as if they had been knocked down. That is violence in its hidden form. And inevitably there is a reaction to it, especially by the young whose energies and ambitions are being blocked. Much of today's visible violence is the inevitable response to society's invisible violence. It is salutary sometimes to ponder the question: 'Who are the instigators of violence – the rampaging mob on the street or the comfortable members of society who forced them there?' As

we watch the pictures of rioting youngsters on our TVs should we not ask: 'who started this – the youngsters out there or we who sit in our comfortable homes, satisfied and fulfilled?'

(3) *A worldwide loss of understanding of the basic purpose of our life.* 'What will anyone gain by winning the whole world at the cost of his life . . .?' said Jesus (*Matthew 16:26*). Those words seem to me to pinpoint the sickness that affects the world, especially the most technologically advanced nations; it is the desire to 'win the whole world' – to have it all in your power. The great strides made in science and technology in this and the last centuries have engendered a spirit in most of us which makes us want to control things – and people. So we all seek as much power as possible and have a strong dislike of being subject to anything or anybody. This has had its good side. The Trade Union movement began because working men realised they were being crushed by the 'hidden violence' of big industrial concerns. But so often it has led, not to closer cooperation between management and men, but to increasing enmity and suspicion. Power has led us to look at our fellow men and women not as fellow-pilgrims on the journey of life but as opponents.

Similarly, our mastery over so much of the natural world has led us not to wonder at the gift given us of partnership with nature, but to become ruthless exploiters of it. Children are taught to treat all strangers with suspicion; gang-warfare between one group of like-minded people and another is the accepted thing; 'get what you can and the devil take the hind-most' is the order of the day. To quote Tournier again, 'The whole of the history of the last few centuries has been a matter of power. Man has become intoxicated with his growing power. Yes, great victories, the development of science, of technology, of economics; and in the realm of thought, the triumph of rationalism and of the dialectic which sweeps away every contradiction . . . On such a glorious road the concept of the power of God was singularly embarrassing, and therefore it was challenged. We even hear now of the death of God.'[2] So this power, this energy, which is a natural part of our make-up, has been used to possess. *Having* becomes more important than being. Your worth as a person is increased not in what you are in character but in the size of your bank balance.

The Christian answer

Christianity has a tremendous message to offer in the present situation: the proclamation ever more clearly of the Power of God – which is the Power of Love, which, if accepted, will break down self-centred actions. It means the seeking for community, caring for the poor and weak, the re-creation of a prior ideal of service, washing one another's feet. This is to discover one's 'true self' – one's 'soul' – in contrast to 'winning the whole world'. When that happens there will be a transformation of ends and aims and actions. I like the story in Bruce Kenrick's *Come out of the Wilderness*[3] which tells of a Christian group who do their work and witness in the heart of the notorious East Harlem, New York. A gang of young men who have been bent on destruction are impressed by the Christian group's work, and catch a new vision. The gang-leader comes to a storekeeper, a member of the church, and says awkwardly: 'Say, there's something we gotta say'. The storekeeper knows this gang. He replies warily: 'You come to take me away?' The leader goes on: 'It's this way . . . we kinda need some help. You see, we wanna go social.' 'Social?' says the other, 'did you say *social*?' After a time the young men's sincerity is accepted. They give their energies to helping repair the church building. They become a tremendous asset in the church's work. They had ceased to be a violent gang; they 'went social'. They used just as much energy, just as much vigour and attacking power, but now it was positive and not negative, it was for the sake of the community, not in rebellion against it.

It may be a very broad interpretation of the word, but can we not say that there is a 'violence' which is good – the violence of love, the aggressiveness of caring? If this interpretation is valid we can go on to say that Jesus was the most violent character in history! He fought; he fought hypocrisy, he fought materialism, he fought all that depersonalises, he fought all that separates humans from one another, from nature – from God. He fought sin – which is that which separates us from the love of God. It was a war he never gave up. And paradoxical as it may seem, he displayed his most violent attack in letting himself be crucified; he attacked death itself by his acceptance of it. And he won.

The Christian task today is what it has always been – to try to bring about a change in humanity's understanding of what is the purpose of that power, that driving-force, that is the essence of living. It is to change our relationship to our fellows from hostility to reconciliation, from a desire to dominate to genuine love. We are members one of another. Hence the importance of our various church fellowships, groups of all kinds in which we learn to trust one another, to be open to one another, to be that Body in which all the members have their essential part to play for the health of the whole. Paul puts it so clearly in *1 Corinthians 12:14–26*. Hence, too, the importance of organising young people's groups of all kinds, from toddlers' play-groups to teenagers' discussion groups in our churches and outside them; it is in them that the youngsters' energies are transformed from violent destructiveness to dynamic caring.

And, difficult as it may be, this is our contribution as a Christian community to the wider world of industrial, racial and international relations. It can be done. It has been done all over the world where the spirit of Christ has been portrayed and recognised and accepted. This is the gospel of reconciliation – the whole meaning of our Faith.

References

1. Paul Tournier (1978), *The Violence Inside*, p. 6. SCM Press Ltd., London.
2. Page 179 of the above publication.
3. Bruce Kenrick (1962) *Come out of the Wilderness*, p. 186. Fontana (HarperCollins Publishers), London.

Questions for Discussion

1. Do you consider that our present society is growing more violent? If so, in what ways and why?
2. Discuss the suggestion that violence is actually a perversion of a necessary and good quality in human nature. Could it be said that all sins are corruptions of God-given energies?

12. Conclusion

There are so many other urgent matters that need the modern Christian's attention. But in a short book like this they have to be omitted. There is, for example, the problem of *Poverty in a Wealthy World*, the gulf between the well-off in our country and the poverty-stricken, the unemployed and the homeless; the gulf between the northern hemisphere and the southern. Why do so many Africans teeter on the edge of starvation? Where are justice and mercy today? A fresh look at the Old Testament Prophets and the teaching of Jesus's Sermon on the Mount might help us here.

But a small book must end here. I repeat my reason for writing all this. It is because of my conviction that although many splendid books have been written on all the subjects touched upon, I often feel that the rank and file Christians are not being given the opportunity and the challenge to talk about them.

What I have written may have left some baffled and feeling there is nothing left any more that we can be absolutely sure about. So I end by asking: what *can* we be sure of in this challenging, complicated time? We can, as Christians, be sure of God, the God who has spoken, and continues to speak to us through all things and many great prophets and, we believe, most clearly of all through the life, teaching, death and resurrection of Jesus Christ. So we can be sure of the ultimate reality of Love, as the foundation of the universe and the ultimate law of all human relationships. Sure? Well, indeed, it is the sureness of faith. And faith is something we have to put into action. Accept it, assume it is true, test it – and see what happens. And in all our discussing and questioning, what happens to the Jesus portrayed in the Gospels? I believe we begin to see more deeply into the meaning of what he taught and did. He said to his friends: 'There is much more that I could say to you, but the burden would be too great for you now. However, when the Spirit of truth comes, he will guide you into all the truth . . .' (*John 16:12–13*). That promise of his has been fulfilled again and again through many centuries. It continues to be fulfilled in ours.

Suggestions for Further Reading

John Bowden (1988), *Jesus, the Unanswered Questions*. SCM Press Ltd., London.

Sheila Cassidy (1988), *Sharing the Darkness – the Spirituality of Caring*. Darton, Longman and Todd, London.

Churches Together in Pilgrimage (1989). British Council of Churches & The Catholic Truth Society, London.

Jack Dominian (1984), *Make or Break (An Introduction to Marriage Counselling)*. SPCK, London.

Jack Dominian (1987), *Sexual Integrity*. Darton, Longman and Todd, London.

Shirley du Boulay (1984), *Cecily Saunders – the Founder of the Modern Hospice Movement*. Hodder & Stoughton, London.

Christopher Lamb (1985), *Belief in a Mixed Society*. Lion Publishing plc, Oxford.

The Myth of Christian Uniqueness (1988), Ed by Hick and Knitter. SCM Press Ltd., London.

Alan Race (1983), *Christians and Religious Pluralism*. SCM Press Ltd., London.

Bryan Rippin (1985), *The Christian Juggler*. Epworth Press, London.

R. J. Sider (1977), *Rich Christians in an Age of Hunger*. Hodder & Stoughton Ltd., London.

Peter Stow and Mike Fearon (1987), *Youth in The City*. Hodder & Stoughton Ltd., London.

The Methodist Church, Division of Social Responsibility, publishes a number of useful reports, pamphlets and books on many of the topics discussed in this book. Write to them for details:

Division of Social Responsibility,
Methodist Church,
1 Central Buildings,
Westminster,
London SW1H 9NH